Maximillien de

2022

THE RETURN OF THE EXTRATERRESTRIAL ANUNNAKI

Based upon
The Anunnaki Final Warning to Humanity, the End
of Time, and the Return of the Anunnaki in 2022.
8th Edition

TIMES SQUARE PRESS
New York

2022
The Return of the Extraterrestrial Anunnaki

Based upon
The Anunnaki Final Warning to Humanity, the End of Time, and the Return of the Anunnaki in 2022.
8th Edition. Revised and Condensed

Maximillien de Lafayette

TIMES SQUARE PRESS

New York
2012

From the Mouzakraat of Sinhar Marduchk*
Announcing the return of the Anunnaki to Earth

From Ana'kh, the Anunnaki language:
1. Michrachk Sinhar Anunna Ila Erdu Ina Kitbani Nouru Ilmu
2. Wa Tahiriim kiblah-ra Michrachki
3. Ana mia "Maiyaa" inaduu nisa khalkah

Translation
1. [The] Return of the Lords Anunnaki to Earth is written in the Light of Knowledge
2. And the Purified shall prepare my return
3. In the waters shall cast a new creation

Translated from Ana'kh to English by Maximillien de Lafayette, Cairo, 1962.

***   ***   ***

Linguistic notes:

a-Mouzakraat means records, notes or diary in Ana'kh, the language of the Anunnaki. In ancient and modern Arabic, the word Mouzakaraat means memoirs. And the word "Zikr" means memory or remembrance.

b-Sinhar means lord.

c-Anunna means Anunnaki. It is a linguistic variation of the words "Anunnaki" and "Anaki", in their archaic use by the ancient Semites, Arwadians and Phoenicians. The Hebrew word Anakim and the ancient Hyksos term/name Anuramkim mean the same thing.
Other names of the Anunnaki:

* Mouzakraat of Sinhar Marduchk shall be published soon. It is the world's first authentic Anunnaki's manuscript provided by an Anunnaki Sinhar.

The Anunnaki were known to many neighboring countries in the Near East, Middle East, and Anatolia. Because of the languages' differences, the Anunnaki were called differently.

For instance:
- **1**-The Habiru (Early Hebrews/Israelites) called them Nephilim, meaning to fall down to earth, as well as Anakim.

- **2**-Some passages in the Old Testament refer to them as Elohim.

- **3**-In Ashuric (Assyrian-Chaldean), and Syriac-Aramaic, they are called Jabaariyn, meaning the mighty ones.

- **4**-In Aramaic, Chaldean and Hebrew, the Anunnaki as Gibborim mean the mighty or majestic ones.

- **5**-In literary Arabic, it is Jababira. The early Arabs called them Al Jababira; sometimes Amalika.

- **6**-The Egyptians called them Neteru.

- **7**-The early Phoenicians called them An.Na Kim, meaning the god or heaven who sent them to us.

- **8**-The early inhabitants of Arwad called then Anu.ki, meaning the subjects or followers of Anu. Sometimes, they were called Anu. Ki.ram. (Ram means people, persons, community, tribes, group)

- **9**-The early Hyskos (Ancestors of the Armenians) who invaded and ruled Egypt for more than 300 years, called them the Anuramkir and Anuramkim, meaning the people of Anu on earth. It is composed of three words: Anu + ram (People) + Ki (Earth). The primitive form of Ki was kir or kiim.

- **10-**The Greeks called them the Annodoti.

- **11-**In the Book of Enoch, they are called The Nephilim, "The Sons of God," or the "Watchers".

- **12-**The Ulema call them Annakh or Al Annaki, meaning the people from above.

- **13-**In other parts of Anatolia, and especially in the lands of the Hittites, the Anunnaki were also called Anunnaku, and Ananaki.

d-Erdu means planet Earth.
Ard in Arabic.
Heretz in Hebrew.
Erda, Irdi in proto-Phoenician, Ugaritic.

e-Kitbani means written. Kitaba is a document or a book (Conic Inscriptions) in Ana'kh.
Kitab in Arabic, and a variation of Ketab in ancient Turkish, Farsi and Urdu. All these words were directly derived from the Anunnaki language.

f-Nouru means light.
From this Anunnaki's word derived numerous words included in the languages of the ancient and modern Near East and Middle East.
For instance the word Nour appears in Arabic, Urdu, Turkish, Farsi and several ancient languages. Even the Judaic/Hebrew word Menora is closely related to Nouru.

g-Tahiriim means the Purified Ones, sometime it refers to the Ascended Masters, which are one of the two highest categories of the Anunnaki-Ulema.

h-Mia "Maiyaa" means water.
Mia or Mie appeared in the ancient Assyrian texts, as well as in the Akkadian/Sumerian inscriptions of Tiglath Pileser.
In Pre-Islamic and modern Arabic, it is Maii or Ma'.
In Phoenician it is Mem.

i-Khalkah means the Creation of Man.
Khalikah in Arabic.

***   ***   ***

Table of Contents

From the Mouzakraat of Sinhar Marduchk...7
Announcing the return of the Anunnaki to Earth...7
Note from the Publishers...23

PART ONE
The Return of the Anunnaki...27

Final warning and the Apocalypse...27

- The Mayan Calendar and other return's dates…28
- How about the 2022 scenario? …29
- What contact? What return?…30
- Why the Anunnaki contact or Anunnaki return is so different and so important on many levels?…32
- Identified cities in India for the return of the Anunnaki…35
- Earth's designated landing areas for the Anunnaki's return to our planet in 2022…35
- Will you be there when the Anunnaki return to earth? Find out! …37
- What are you chances of meeting an Anunnaki? …37
- Here is the formula! Do your math! …37
- The following is an excerpt from a dialogue between a student and an Ulema…37
- Is it true that their return will seal the fate of Planet Earth and all humanity?…39
- Did the Anunnaki plan on returning to Earth to clean house?…39
- Ambar Anati's story and revelations…39
- Sinhar Ambar Anati in her own words…40
- Three members of the NSA were waiting for me…41
- The Grays attended the meeting…41
- Holographic pictures that showed them the entire sequence of the Roswell crash…42
- At the Dulce Base…44
- We were joined by a Gray…46
- The First Level…46
- The Second Level…47
- The Third Level…47
- The Fourth Level…48
- The Fifth, Sixth and Seventh Levels…48
- The Eighth Level…49
- The Ninth Level…49
- The Tenth Level…50

- Grays in shape-shifted form...51
- The Grays and their slaves, the Hybrids, have invaded the world...51
- The Anunnaki Council...53
- The United States military authorities would not cooperate...53
- The Anunnaki needed a planet-sized laboratory...56
- The Anunnaki fostered the evolutionary process...56
- Humanity is divided into three groups, regarding their level of contamination...57
- The first group...58
- The second group...59
- The third group...60
- A cataclysmic event...62
- The Anunnaki's Bubble...62
- Anunnaki guides will be there for the humans...63
- Ba'abs (Star Gates) exist everywhere...64
- The final stage...69
- The final clash...76

Coding and decoding the significance of the year 2022...85

- First interpretation of the Code...85
- Second interpretation of the Code...86
- Characteristics of the number 6...86
- The number 6, carbon and the creation of mankind...86
- The number 6 is one of the six major extraterrestrial hot spots on Earth...87
- Statue of a Phoenician goddess found in Malta...88
- Photo of the ruins of ancient Malta, which is one of the six major extraterrestrial hot spots on Earth...89

- Photo of the ancient walls of Malta...90
- Photo of the ruins of Baalbeck, one of the earliest colonies of the Anunnaki on Earth...91
- Photo of the Trilithon of Baalbeck, part of the early space centers of the Anunnaki in the Near East...91
- Another view of the legendary Trilithon of Baalbeck...92
- Photo of the tomb of Hiram, king of Tyre, founder of the first Freemasonry Rite in the world, and an offspring of the remnants of the Anunnaki in the Near East...93
- Photo of the ruins of the ancient city of Tyre in Phoenicia (Modern day Lebanon). ...94
- Photo of Tyre (Sour) today; a Shiite Muslim city in Southern Lebanon...95
- Photo of the Ziggurat of Nippur....96
- Photo of a tower toward the heavens in Nippur...97
- The Phoenician "Hook"...98
- Meaning of the number 6 in Anunnaki-Phoenician Alphabets...98
- Facts...98

In 1947, a Grays' spacecraft crashed in Roswell...100

- Statement by Ambar Anati on record...101
- On the night of February 20, the President of the United States disappeared...105
- A Cover-up!...106
- It was a cover-up for the President's real business...106
- Photo of Muroc Field/ Edwards Air Force Base...108
- How was this meeting arranged, in the first place?...109
- Before the meetings: Two major black projects...109
- Second meeting in 1954...110

- United States "Protocol on Extraterrestrials' visit to Earth in 2022"...111
- Master Kanazawa's Kira'at (An excerpt)...112
- Some of the issues discussed in the protocol and the manual are...113
- United States Government publications on extraterrestrial invasions...115
- 1-Government alien invasion plan...115
- 2-Government publications on aliens and security...116
- 3-The US government's plan with Aliens...133
- 4-United States National Defense Against Aliens' Invasion...116
- 5-Aliens' attack plan...116
- 6-What to do in case of an alien attack...116

*** *** ***

PART TWO
The Return of the Anunnaki: Q&A...117

Outlook for mankind after 2022...119
- Question: What is the outlook for mankind after the year 2022? ...119
- You have explained this in some detail in your books but will we live in peace or does humankind still pose a threat to one another if challenges and greed are proposed like they always have been?...119
- Answer...119

Another extraterrestrial threat other than the Gray's aliens...119

- Question: After the Anunnaki's job is finished here on earth through decontamination will we ever have to deal with another extraterrestrial threat other than the Gray's aliens?...118
- Answer...119

On aliens competing with the Anunnaki to rule our planet...119

- Question: Are there any other alien races in this galaxy or another that could compete with the superstar status of the Anunnaki and rule our planet?...119
- Answer...119

Would the Anunnaki come to aid the planet if another alien threat happens?...119

- Question: You have said that the Anunnaki feel responsible for the hybrid contamination between the humans and the Gray's, would the Anunnaki ever come to the aid of the planet again if this threat would happen?...119
- Answer...119
- Question: Has the planet ever come close to another threat as serious as the Gray's and will it be a possibility?...120
- Answer...120

Hybrid Grays: Adoption and DNA contamination...120

- Question: Have there been a large number of ones that were disease free and human enough to be adopted?...120
- Answer...120

- Question: Could someone have a relative hybrid or be a child of a hybrid and not know it?... 120
- Answer...120
- Question: I always wonder how people with no compassion what-so-ever are the same species. It seems that living as a loving and compassionate being is what our natural instinct wants us to do, so I wonder if hybrids have any connection to emotionless behavior? ...120
- Answer...120
- Question: I have read the discussions about contaminated DNA and am curious to know if it is to the point where large amounts of people have some connection to hybrids?... 120
- Answer...120
- Question: Is it true that hybrid human/grey babies and children are being created and raised in secret bases?... 120
- What of the stories of horrific experiments being performed on abducted humans in labs by the Greys as part of their breeding/tissue harvesting programs?... 120
- Answer...120
- Question: What is the reason behind the Greys interbreeding program with humans?... 120
- Answer...120
- Question: Is one of these Anunnaki Gods going to take over the earth after the pole shift?... 120
- Answer...120
- Questions: I am very worried by what you have written on the subject of the return of the Anunnaki in 2022? Is it for real?...121
- Are they going to change the way we look?... 121
- Are they going to get rid of us and replace us with a new human race?
- What kind?... 121

- Answer...121
- Question: Will the Anunnaki intervene to prevent possible use of atomic/thermonuclear weapons prior to, or during their return in 2022?... 121
- Answer...121

Who will survive the return of the extraterrestrial Anunnaki? 121

- Question: What percentage of the world's population will survive the return of the Anunnaki to become part of the new human race after 2022?... 121
- Answer...121

How many other Anunnaki will be part of the return? ...121

- Question: Though the return will be led by Sinhars Marduchk and Inannaschamra, how many other Anunnaki will be part of the return? ...121
- And how many Anunnaki guides will there be, for humans who will be saved and returned to earth after the cleansing?...121
- Answer...121

Anunnaki efficient energy systems ...121

- Question: What kind of clean and efficient energy systems, and modes of transportation will the Anunnaki introduce after 2022?...200
- Answer...121

Stargate over Chicago...221

- Question: Is there a stargate/ba'ab in Chicago?...122
- Where exactly is it located, and what does it look like? How would you jump into a ba'ab?...122

- Terminal of Grand Central Station in downtown Chicago...122
- Answer...122

***   ***   ***

Note from the Publishers

The great Babylonian king Hammurabi, the sixth monarch of the first Babylonian dynasty. Hammurabi received his Code from the Anunnaki.

Maximillien de Lafayette's book "Anunnaki Final Warning" was sold out and no longer available.
We approached him with the idea of updating and rewriting a new edition of this book, with the intention of bringing to the reader, knowledge and information never before released to the public, and source material taken directly from Maximillien de Lafayette's work and the Ulema Anunnaki Kira'at.

This book contains brand new material as well as new questions and answers and revelations on the return of the Anunnaki in meticulous details.
Please note that the ideas and information within these pages are strictly and solely that of Maximillien de Lafayette and the Ulema, as previously published in his books.
No bibliography has been used or recommended, as no other authors have disserted on this subject.

This book, and all subsequent publications will exclusively contain the original work of Maximillien de Lafayette and the Ulema.

No reference to any other author's book, or use of any other source material will ever be included in our publications, except for short inclusions of governmental data when is permitted and part of the public domain, such as government press releases and information obtained through Freedom of information Act requests.

*** *** ***

PART ONE

The Return of the Anunnaki
Final warning and the Apocalypse

The Return of the Anunnaki
Final warning and the Apocalypse

The Mayan Calendar and other return dates

> 2012 marks the end of the Mayan calendar. It has no relation whatsoever to the return of the Anunnaki. Any proposed theory pertaining to this date is not backed up by science.
> Such assumption is pseudoscience.
> Mr. Burak Eldem was the first writer to suggest that the Anunnaki will return in 2012. Again, this "assigned" date could not be backed by astronomy or any other science.
> It is evident that people are confusing the Mayan calendar that ends in 2012 with the Anunnaki return or intention to return.

Some authors have suggested that the Mayas and the Incas have some sort of link to the Anunnaki, because of their extensive knowledge of astronomy and cosmology.

The same thing was said about the Sumerians who mapped the heavens. Yet, there is no date for their return to earth in the Sumerian and Mayan texts.

According to Mr. Sitchin, the next passage of Nibiru will occur in the year 2085. This means that the Anunnaki will show up in 2085.

Any scientific data to substantiate this idea?
No.

However, Mr. Sitchin must have his own reasons and logic for advancing such a theory. On what foundation did he cement his assumption? I don't know.

I respect the man and admire his pioneering work. But, I have no clues as to how Mr. Sitchin came up with this date.

***   ***   ***

How about the 2022 scenario?
The only reference made to the date 2022 was found in the Ulema manuscript called "The Book of Ramadosh."

In essence, the Book of RamaDosh is a cosmological-metaphysical-philosophical work based upon science, astronomy and quantum physics.
Yet, at the time it was written or compiled, quantum physics theories did not exist.
How the Ulema knew about quantum physics, and anti-gravity laws, remains an unsolved mystery, unless you are one of their adepts.
The "Book of Ramadosh" and the book "Ilmu Al Donia" described *ad infinitum* the return of the Anunnaki to Earth, and their plan for humanity.
According to two Anunnaki-Ulema, Masters, Ambar Anati, and Maximillien de Lafayette, the Anunnaki's return has already been announced to leading figures in several countries. Some have suggested that India was chosen as the landing terminal of the Anunnaki.

*** *** ***

Numerous ufologists believe that the United States is more likely to be the Anunnaki's return destination.
They claim that American military scientists and a group of astrophysicists at NASA and top-echelon officials at the NSA have learned about the Anunnaki's return (Including the date of their return) from an extraterrestrial race currently living on Earth.
Some of these extraterrestrials work at the Dulce base, AUTEC, and other underground facilities in Arizona, Nevada, Puerto Rico and Mexico.
How accurate are these claims?
Nobody knows for sure.

However, this could be quite accurate, simply because the Greys who live on Earth and underwater already know that the Anunnaki are planning on returning to Earth.
And since the Greys are working on several joint-projects with some very powerful governments, one can assume that they have informed our governments about the Anunnaki's return.

In addition, a few years ago, in Washington, D.C., an Anunnaki Sinhar by the name of Ambar Anati had two meetings with top officials and leading figures in science, and informed them that the return of the Anunnaki is "irrevocable", because the Greys have contaminated the human race."

In the area of speculation and rhetoric, we have 3 proposed dates, so far:

- 1-According to Z. Sitchin, the return of the Anunnaki shall occur sometime in 2085.
- 2-According to independent researchers and "fans" of the Mayan Calendar, the Anunnaki will return in 2012 and this could change humanity's fate, and bring the world to a catastrophic end.
- 3-According to the Ulema, the precise date is 2022.

*** *** ***

What Contact?
What Return?

The return of the Anunnaki triggers enormous global interest, and excites the imagination of people.
The reasons?
Well, the list of reasons is *ad infinitum*...endless. According to our readers, the return of the Anunnaki could:

(a) Change their religious belief systems;
(b) Alter the fabric of our societies;
(c) Clean-up mind and body contamination;
(d) Establish cosmic order.

Highly cultured researchers (debunkers and believers alike) have begun to express an increased and intense interest in this topic, because the possibility of contacting extraterrestrials, and/or being contacted by them has become a possibility that science can no longer refute or deny.

The paramount questions rotating around the Anunnaki's return are:
1-When?
2-How?
3-Where?
3-For what purpose?
4-And who will be contacted on earth? Heads of governments and important people only, or just, you and me, and the rest of us?

Basically, those are the major concerns.

However, contact with extraterrestrials is neither the main topic, nor the primordial concern per se, because several scientific groups and secret military units are already working in sync with various alien races.

Many top echelon military men and the crème de la crème of scientists in the United States have already confirmed such cooperation.

The main theme is not "Extraterrestrial Contact", but a contact with the Anunnaki. And this difference is extremely important and major on so many levels.

***   ***   ***

Why the Anunnaki contact or Anunnaki return is so different and so important on many levels?

- 1-History shows, that there is a special (and very unique) relationship between the Anunnaki and the human race.

Unlike other extraterrestrial races that interact with us for very specified and specific purposes, such as abduction of humans in exchange for alien technology, or peaceful co-habitation/co-occupation of planet earth via a mutual agreement/protocol, the Anunnaki:
  (a) Do not interact with us,
  (b) Do not abduct humans,
  (c) Do not cooperate with United States military scientists.

The Anunnaki do not need the consent of humans to carry on their projects, and/or to coordinate mutual operations. They had, and still have full control over us from the dawn of the creation of the primitive humans.

We function, think, act and react according to what they have installed in our "Intellect program", genes, DNA, and "Mental Conduit".

They created us genetically.

Other extraterrestrial races currently working with top military scientists on earth have control over earth and its inhabitants because of their far advanced technology.
These alien races operate very differently from the Anunnaki.
Their agenda is macabre, for it contains:

- (a) Human abduction;
- (b) Animal mutilation;
- (c) Genetic experiments;
- (d) Mind control;
- (e) Territorial ambitions.

The Anunnaki have no interest whatsoever in dominating the earth and controlling our minds.
The Anunnaki have already created our mental faculties and "programmed" us some 65,000 years ago. Thus, their physical interference in human affairs is not necessary at all.

- 2-The Anunnaki left earth thousands of years ago. Many other alien races are still on earth carrying out their own programs and projects. For a multitude of reasons, they need planet earth as a spatial/terrestrial base.

The Anunnaki (Or Igigi) do not need planet earth as a base for their galactic enterprises.
They lived here, created multiple human races, founded cities, established religions and taught us how to think, how to act and how to understand our physical world. Their job is done!

The Anunnaki are no longer interested in human affairs, because the human race has nothing particular or beneficial to offer to the Anunnaki. But other extraterrestrial races are in extreme need of using humans in any capacity, role, function, and aspect to carry out their operations. Ufologists and scholars know very well the complete scenario and agenda of alien races currently living on earth. We have plenty of theories and hypotheses, but nothing is absolutely certain.

- 3-Almost 99.99% of extraterrestrial activities, sightings, landings, human abductions, visitations, encounters and contacts occur, develop, and materialize in the sphere-existence of various alien races living on earth, but never in the Anunnaki's sphere or perimeter.

The Anunnaki are not part of this spectrum. In other words, the Anunnaki are out of the picture. They left earth thousands of years ago, and are not very much interested in us.

Thus, a return of the Anunnaki to earth is an exceptional event in the history of mankind. Very unique and very significant indeed.

> The Anunnaki must have serious, paramount and indispensable reasons for returning to planet earth.
> Other alien races are here on earth. Some left, while many others are still working and living in secret military bases, laboratories on the surface of the earth, underwater and in terrestrial orbit.
> So, there is nothing new or special about their presence on earth. But the return of the Anunnaki to earth is evidently very special, and constitutes a major event.
> The Anunnaki are not coming back to mine gold!!! This is an old silly story we will not bother with.
> The Anunnaki must have more important and predominant reasons for their return. And this is what makes their anticipated return extremely paramount and significant! This book explores and explains the scope, nature and reasons for the return of the Anunnaki.

*** *** ***

Identified cities in India for the return of the Anunnaki

Some writers have suggested that India was chosen as the landing "terminal." Those suggestions have appeared on many websites, and in articles published by journalists from India. The early and very ancient Anunnaki-Ulema manuscripts identified the "Hind and Sindh" (Ancient territories of modern India and Pakistan) as one of the landing spots for the return of the Anunnaki.

The most frequently mentioned cities and regions for the landing of the Anunnaki are:

- 1-Punjab,
- 2-State of Multan also called Bayt al-Zahab by the Arabs, and Dar Al-Aman by the Mughals,
- 3-Lamghan,
- 4-The area surrounding the river of Chinab,
- 5-Kashmir,
- 6-Jazirat Al Sind.

*** *** ***

Earth's designated landing areas for the Anunnaki's return to our planet in 2022

Cheik Al Mutawalli and Dr. Farid Tayarah (Both, members of Hiram Masonic Lodges in Lebanon and Egypt, and custodians of the Book "Sun of the Great Knowledge": Shams Al Maa-Ref Al Koubra) said that some regions of India lign up perfectly with the "Anunnaki Triangle" that defines precisely the perimeter of their landing and designated cities for their return.

This "Triangle" encompasses additional cities outside India. Dr. Tayarah named those cities and areas:

Aktion,	Bijjeh,	Geilenkirchen,
Alaska,	Brazilia,	Gyumri,
Amchit,	Bucharest,	Honolulu,
Amrit,	California,	Kamishli,
Antioch,	Carthage,	Kent,
Arizona,	Cherbough,	Konya,
Arwad,	Dover,	Le Havre,
Baalbeck,	Dushanbe,	London,
Basra,	Gabala,	Malta,
Mexico City,	Paris,	Trapani,
Nevada,	Prague,	Tyre,
New Mexico,	Puerto Rico,	Ur,
New York City,	Saint Petersburg,	Vera Cruz,
Niederheid,	Sidon,	Washington DC
Oerland,	Texas,	

Will you be there when the Anunnaki return to earth? Find out!

**Will you be there when the Anunnaki return to earth? Find out!
What are you chances of meeting an Anunnaki? Here is the formula!
DO YOUR MATH!**

*** *** ***

The following is an excerpt from a dialogue between a student and an Ulema:

The student asked the Ulema: "Well, if I correctly use these numbers, would I be able to learn more about the return of the Anunnaki? Are they a threat to us? Can I meet the Anunnaki?"

The Ulema replied: "First, the Anunnaki are a threat only to the "Fasidin" (Bad people, rotten people in his language). So you have nothing to fear for yourself…Yes, the numbers will tell you a lot about the Anunnaki."
He stopped for a few seconds, and then, said: 'Tayeb Esma'h (OK, listen now, in his language), when you have some free time…and if you are interested in knowing if you have any chance of seeing with your own eyes the "Roujou'h" (Arrival) of the Anunnaki, do this…consider it as a game for now…nothing serious…just play with these numbers, and see what you could find…OK?
Do this:
- Write down the number 2022
- Add your age to 2022
- Subtract 6
- Deduct 14 from what you got
- Add together the four digits of the new number you got
- Add the new number to form one single digit
- Add the digit you got to 2022

He continued: "The final number you get will tell you if you are going to be one of those lucky persons who will be blessed by the Anunnaki…remember blessing is not a religious benediction or a spiritual blessing…no…no...no…it is simply your chance to enter a new age of happiness, tranquility and an enormous personal satisfaction. Do the numbers, see if you will be around…"

The student did not quite understand how the final number will tell him about all that? So he asked the learned one: "How would I understand what the final number means?"
The Ulema replied: "You will, just compare the number to the year 2022…if your number is under 2022, you are not a lucky man…if your number is equal or higher, then you have made it…you will be there, you will meet them and your life will be full of happiness…"

Anxiously, the student asked his teacher: "So, If I get less than 2022…I am screwed! Right?" The Ulema laughed and replied: "Not totally, try again…be patient…take your time, and if the same number pops again, do not panic, add to the number, the numerical value of the Phoenician letter "Aleph"…" (First letter of the Phoenician, Aramaic, Hebrew, Anunnaki, and Arabic alphabets.)

*** *** ***

Is it true that their return will seal the fate of Planet Earth and all humanity?

Question:
Did the Anunnaki plan on returning to Earth to clean house?
Is it true that their return will seal the fate of Planet Earth and all humanity?

Answer:
Absolutely!
According to Sinhar Anbar Anati – an Anunnaki hybrid woman born on Earth of Anunnaki lineage, who married an Anunnaki Sinhar, traveled to Nibiru (Ashtari), lived there for several years, and studied the true history of humanity here on earth as well as learning much about life on Nibiru – YES they will be returning in 2022, and the decision they have made is now irrevocable and final.

Before her final departure from Earth back to Nibiru in 2007, Sinhar Anbar Anati contacted Ulema de Lafayette with a desire for him to publish an account of her life and experiences both here on Earth and Nibiru, with humans, Anunnaki, hybrids and Greys.
The most fascinating parts of her account were her meetings with top echelon military brass and scientists from different countries and governments, concerning the return of the Anunnaki to Earth, and the reason behind their return.

*** *** ***

Ambar Anati's story and revelations:

Herewith is an exerpt from her story, as told to Maximillien de Lafayette and Dr. Ilil Arbel, who included it in their book "Anunnaki Ultimatum End of Time."

Note: With Dr. Anbel, I wrote the story of Sinhar Ambar Anati in 2008.
The following is an excerpt from the story, and it has been authorized by Ulema and author de Lafayette to reproduce it in this book, in its entirety.

Sinhar Ambar Anati in her own words:

I was taken to earth, and went to a hotel in New York. I had with me a special device, an ingenious thing that had on it the special telephone numbers of top members of the National Security Agency, or NSA as everyone refers to them. Only two or three people in the world have these numbers, not even the president of the United States has access to them.

They are used only for matters related to extra terrestrial reverse engineering. The device makes sure the phones will be promptly answered, and when I called, I gave them data that they recognized as their own extraterrestrial material.

They were shocked, but nevertheless they agree to meet with me. I suppose they realized they had no choice.

Rather politely, they offered to fly me to Washington DC, where they wanted to have the meeting, but I informed them that it was not necessary.

It was easy for me to simply materialize in D.C., and I did not want them to know my current address, if this could be prevented. They directed me to come to the Four Seasons Hotel in Georgetown, where they were to meet me at the lobby.

I was to know, if questioned at the hotel, that I was heading for the suite that was reserved under the name of a Middle Eastern gentleman who owned a limousine service in D.C., and had often used the hotel for similar purposes.

*** *** ***

Three members of the NSA were waiting for me

I materialized a little distance away from the hotel, and walked there on M Street.

Three members of the NSA were waiting for me, and they took me to the reserved suite, where fifteen more people were sitting around a huge table.

They rose and greeted me politely, but I could clearly see the suspicion in their eyes and in their thoughts.

I noticed that the shades of all the windows were closed, and I saw no telephones. However, they all had gadgets in their hands which I have recognized immediately.

They were navigation devices, which at the time were known only to extraterrestrials, not to any humans.

For a moment I assumed that they got it from the Grays, for communication purposes, and then noticed that quite a few of these people were really Grays who had shape-shifted to resemble humans.

I can easily identify them, because even while shape-shifting, the Grays cannot turn their heads independently of their body. They have to turn the entire body if they wish to look to the sides. As they turn, their eyes cannot follow their heads quickly, like humans' eyes, but they have to refocus.

*** *** ***

The Grays attended the meeting.

All that is done rather discretely, but after living with the Hybrids and the Grays, I could not miss that.

In addition, humans usually fidget, move around. The Grays never do. When seated, they sit quietly, immobile.

When standing, they are straight and immobile as well. In addition to that, I had more instructions from Nibiru as to how to recognize all shape-shifters, which I cannot explain because it involves using the Conduit.

One of the Grays at the end of the table was tapping nervously on the edge of the table with something that looked like a pen, and from time to time pointed it towards me.

I recognized this gadget as a scanning device, such as we use on Nibiru. It was not held by any of the humans, because this fiber/scanning device was not known to the humans' scientific community until much later, 2006 or 2007. I supposed the Grays kept it to themselves for a while.

I did my best to ignore the fact that half the people there were Grays, and proceeded as if I had no idea and was talking only to humans.

I had nothing to fear, really, since I could annihilate the Grays with one thought, and I decided that discretion was the best approach. The Grays maintained their pretence throughout it, and I said nothing at all.

Come to think of it, I was used to the treachery of the Grays, but I have to admit I was a little distressed by the humans' duplicity and stupidity.

Did they really think I won't recognize the Grays?

*** *** ***

Holographic pictures that showed them the entire sequence of the Roswell crash.

I have explained to them who I was, telling the absolute truth, and giving my name as Ambar Anati. Naturally they did not believe me. To help persuade them, I first of all projected certain images on one of the walls.

These were holographic pictures that showed them the entire sequence of the Roswell crash, where the Gray was held, and data pertaining to their research.

They still were not persuaded that I was who I claimed to be, but the fact that the projections were done without any equipment made them uneasy and less sure of themselves.
They were at least ready to listen.

I told them quite a lot about the Grays and their agenda. "By now," I said, "you must be aware that they do not tell the truth, that they are not to be trusted."

"Business is business," said one of them. "They have given us more than they promised, too, so we have gained additional knowledge.
It's not really a big deal if they abduct a few more people."

"First of all, it is not a few people. It's thousands that are tortured and killed."

"What can we say?" answered another. "Sometimes harsh measures cannot be avoided." I did my best to hide my feelings about such a statement, and went on.

"Are you aware of the fact that they are trying to take over earth?"

"No, we were not informed about such intent," said another.

"And are you aware of the invisible radio plasmic belt around earth? They want to isolate earth from the universe. This belt can expand up or down, and can affect missiles, rockets, or airplanes, and blow them up. It explains what has happened to various airplanes in Vietnam, and also to human spacecrafts and space missions."

"We don't understand what you want us to do," said one of them.

"I want you to trust the Anunnaki. They intend to help you get rid of the Grays. This is really very simple. Either you go with the Anunnaki, in which case much can be done, or you stay with the Grays.
If you choose to stay with the Grays, the Anunnaki will return and clean up the earth, in a way that you will not like. They are perfectly capable of annihilating the entire population if the atrocities do not stop."

"Are you threatening us?" asked one of them. The rest stared at me, impassive.

"I would not call it a threat," I said. "I would call it a fair warning.

Remember, the Anunnaki are stronger than both humans and Grays.

They did not have to send me, they could do what they wanted without warning. But they prefer to save as many humans as possible."

"How do we know how strong the Anunnaki really are?" said one of them. "After all, they have been away for so long. They don't seem to have much of an interest in us."

"Let me show you a small example of what the Anunnaki can do," I said.

In a blink, I multiplied myself into thirty Victorias; we arranged ourselves around the table, behind the sitting people. They jumped off their seats, shocked.

"It's a trick," cried some of them. "Grab her!"

"Please, do grab," I said. "Touch all thirty of me, and see that this is not an idle trick. We can become billions, if we wish." Hesitantly, they touched some of the multiples. A few multiples offered to shake hands, which the humans did, trembling. They could not deny the multiple's tangible presence.

I contracted myself into one person again, and sat down. "Please," I said. "I have no desire to frighten you. Sit down and let's be reasonable."

*** *** ***

At the Dulce Base

"Truth is, Ms. Anati," said one of them, "The Grays are an immediate threat. They are right here and we cannot control them. The Anunnaki are far away.

But still, we can see that you wish to help us, and it should be considered. What would you want us to do?"

"I want to start by going into some of the more important places where humans and Grays interact," I said.

"I need much data to deliver to the High Council of Nibiru and receive instructions before I meet the President of the United States, among others."

"I think the best thing to do is to go to Dulce, in New Mexico. It is the most important joint laboratory of the Grays and the U.S. Government," said one of them.

The others nodded in agreement. "There are bases in Nevada, Arizona, and Colorado, among others, but Dulce is the most important."

"Very well. Would you assign one of the members to come with me, act as my escort?" I asked.

"Yes, Colonel X— will go with you." The colonel rose. He seemed to be a respectable, middle-aged man. In reality, he was certainly a Gray. As before, I pretended not to notice.

"Would you like me to materialize you there?" I asked.

"No, I think it's best if we go in a more traditional way," said the colonel. "We don't want to startle the people in Dulce too much. It's best if they don't panic." I agreed and we decided to go the next day, in a military plane.

*** *** ***

On the plane, the colonel, who had become reasonably friendly, gave me some information about Dulce. "It's all underground, you know" he said.

"People know about seven layers, but in truth, there are nine I am aware of, perhaps more I don't even know about. It's really a very large compound."

"Where exactly is it?" I asked.

"It lies under the Archuleta Mesa on the Jicarilla Apache Indian Reservation, near the town of Dulce. Very easy to keep it a secret, the way it is constructed," he said. "And they are very careful about security. You will see."

We finally landed at the small air field. A medium sized building, guarded and surrounded with a high wire fence, stood in the desert. We entered a normal room.

I noticed the cameras in the entrance, and a woman in military uniform looked at some papers Colonel Jones presented to her, but the security was not impressive.

I realized later that the deeper you went into the compound, the stricter the security was.

She pressed a button, and a man came to escort us through a door that led to an escalator.

From then on, it seemed we were descending into Hell.

***   ***   ***

We were joined by a Gray

Everything was clean, shiny, and metallic, much like I remembered from my unpleasant stay with the Hybrids.

No matter where you looked, you saw a security camera. There were side doors everywhere.

Apparently, many secret exits and entrances existed, and each was loaded with security features, some seen, some invisible.

The First Level:

On the first level we were joined by a Gray. He was polite and distant, and showed us into various offices without much comment. The offices were normal, military, and stark. Maps hung on walls, with many pushpins in various colors stuck into them.

The individual colors, the Gray explained, showed sites of high activity of different subjects.

Green, for example, showed sites of heavy spaceship activities, including those of extraterrestrials that were not Grays, and were considered enemies by them.

Red were for areas of cattle mutilation and collection of animal blood. Blue indicated underground activities and caverns. I do not remember all the other colors and sites, but the arrangement was quite elaborate.

The offices were monitored constantly by humans, who wore military-like jumpsuits.

Each carried a gun, quite visibly.

All the uniforms were decorated with the symbol of the Triangle, much like the Phoenician Da (Delta) symbol.

They had various letters and numbers in each triangle, supposedly signifying rank, but I never found out if this was true.

When they saw that we were accompanied by the Gray, they simply ignored us.

*** *** ***

The Second Level:

The second level was exactly the same, full of offices, but after the first level, which we reached by the escalator, we used only elevators.

I was told that the elevators had no cables in them, and were controlled magnetically, using alien technology.

Magnetism also supplied light, which came from flat, round objects, and there were no regular light bulbs in sight.

*** *** ***

The Third Level

The third level was devoted to hospital-like environment used for impregnation of female humans.

I was not allowed into the surgical ward itself, but the Gray explained that the experimenters removed the fetus, and placed it for speeded-up growth in an incubator, creating Hybrids.

In this facility, more than in the one I visited during my previous time with the hybrids, they tended to experiment with genetic manipulation during the very early time in the incubator. The results were quite monstrous sometimes.

Through windows in the walls, I saw cribs, or really a sort of cages, with some of the results.

Deformed humans were the norm – extra arms and legs, small or very large heads, and creatures that did not really look humans. "What do you do with these?" I asked.

"We harvest certain tissues and then kill them," said the Gray. "We learn quite a lot from them about genetics. We apply them to our own research."

*** *** ***

The Fourth Level:

On level four, there were genetic labs that created half human/ half animal creatures.

Their shapes, as I saw them sitting in their cages, were so horrific, that I had to avert my eyes. Some of them had a reptilian look, some had fur, and others looked like gargoyles. "Do you harvest tissues here too?" I asked.

"Yes, we combine this research with the materials we get from the cows. The research is extremely interesting and useful," said the Gray.

*** *** ***

The Fifth, Sixth and Seventh Levels:

The aliens had their living quarters on levels five, six, and seven. These looked much like military barracks, as we passed the corridors and peeked into the rooms, but I saw no reason to enter.

I asked the Gray if it was true that there were additional levels. This did not seem to faze him at all, and he said, in perfect English that seemed so unpleasant, coupled with his scratchy alien voice, that yes, of course there were.

*** *** ***

The Eighth Level:

Apparently, they took advantage of the huge natural caverns under Dulce, and created additional levels. They carried even more security there, and the Gray said that if we wanted to go there, he would have to call two more Grays to accompany us, and we would need to use an eye identification system. These details were quickly accomplished, and we used a side elevator to the eighth level.

Here they also experimented with manipulation of the nervous system by various means.

It allowed them to cause disease and even death from a distance.

"I am afraid you cannot enter the place where the subjects are kept," said the Gray. "These subjects are mostly insane, dangerous, and very susceptible to changes in the routine. If we enter, we might destroy some of the experiments."

*** *** ***

The Ninth Level:

Level nine, where we were invited to enter, contained storage units of fully grown creatures and tissues, in vats, all of them dead. This included tanks full of embryos in various stages of development, waiting for use.

The place was kept as clean, as was the rest of the compound, but the smell of the chemicals was overwhelming. I simply could not stay there long, and Colonel Jones, who until that time showed no emotion, suddenly shape-shifted and appeared in his real, Gray form.

"You knew all along, Ms. Anati," he said, his voice turning scratchy. "I never thought we could trick you, and would have preferred to appear in my true form in the first place, but my group insisted." "It does not signify," I said. "Of course I knew." The other Gray did not pay much attention to the shape-shifting, being used to such practices.

*** *** ***

The Tenth Level:

Level ten, the most secret of them all, was devoted to human aura research, and other extra-sensory abilities, including dreams, hypnosis, etc.

The researchers were able to record dreams on specialized machines; the dreams were studied as part of the major advanced study of psychic power and phenomena.

"Once we are more advanced in this research," said the Gray, "we will have total power over other races. Of course, we mean no harm to humans or to the Anunnaki. We are merely concerned with the Reptilian races."

I almost laughed. No harm to humans? Was the Gray trying to be a PR person?

When we finished our tour, we were escorted out of the complex. The plane was waiting for us outside.

I said nothing about my disgust, horror, and disbelief to anyone. But I had seen enough, and I knew that this was just the tip of the iceberg.

Such treaties must have been entered into by more than just the United States government.

The Grays had reached almost total control over humanity.

*** *** ***

Grays in shape-shifted form

After materializing myself back to New York, I knew I would always be watched, but I also knew how to handle it and avoid my watchers. I needed time.

First, I spent a few days just digesting what I saw.

I made myself invisible, and left the hotel for hours of exploration.

I walked the streets, took the subway, rode on buses, visited museums, stores, offices, hospitals, senior citizens homes, schools, and more.

Everywhere I went I saw Grays in shape-shifted form. Obviously, they did not only infiltrate the military, but spread out much more. They flooded the city.

Some worked in offices, some in restaurants, obviously doing it as part of their agenda.

They were nurses, teachers, officials, sanitation engineers. They were probably doing the same in other cities, urban areas, towns, and even other countries.

*** *** ***

The Grays and their slaves, the Hybrids, have invaded the world

For me, as I mentioned before, it is easy to recognize a shape-shifter. I was taught how to do it by the best teachers on Nibiru. But a human cannot do so very easily. Your doctor could be one. The nice lady in the department store could be one. The teacher of your young child could be one.

In addition, I saw many hybrids.

Vicious, unfeeling, and manipulative, they flocked mostly into the entertainment industry, the financial world, and the advertising field. It seemed they liked glamour.

The Grays and their slaves, the Hybrids, had invaded the world.

After a few days I got to work. Using the same device that had gotten me the telephone numbers of the NSA members, I spent my time contacting and negotiating with hundreds of people from a number of governments on earth.

I also visited other laboratories, bases, and Air Force fields. Every time I negotiated with them, I encountered the same road blocks. Every government on earth was in terror of the Grays.

The Anunnaki were feared, too, and the knowledge that they would very likely attempt to clean the earth, terrified the humans, but not enough to get them out of their fearful paralysis regarding the Grays.

But that was not the worst of it. Unbelievably, many individuals in power simply did not care. All they wanted was to keep their power and control, to wage war. They wanted to make billions and keep it within a tiny group of the financial elite, while the rest of the world was permitted to go to the devil.

*** *** ***

This was a long mission. For years I went from country to country, getting in touch with people in power, acquiring knowledge, collecting data and transferring it, every night, to Nibiru.

The High Council took it all very calmly, and when I despaired, reminded me that my services were invaluable despite the seemingly unachievable goal of converting humanity.

The only bright points of my day were my evening conversations with my daughter and my husband, who were always supportive and loving.

I drudged on and on, until I thought that nothing more could be achieved. I stayed until late 2007, and then I made the call and requested permission to go back to Nibiru, and make my final report.

As always, Marduchk was there for me and I left an earth I no longer loved. I was going home.

*** *** ***

The Anunnaki Council

I report to the Council about my years of envoyship, and I view the frightening plans for the cleansing of the earth before the return of the Anunnaki and their plans for the complete change of the earth.

The years of envoyship have taken their toll on me. I was tired, discouraged, and worse, I began to feel old. It did not show in my appearance, which was a good thing, but I was no longer the strong young woman I used to be.

This time, putting the results of my mission before the High Council, and letting go of the burden and putting it on stronger shoulders, would be a relief.

I was not at all nervous about meeting the Council. I knew that I had done all I could, and more than that I could not do – unless the Council thought that there was more to accomplish. If they did, I would most certainly obey.

*** *** ***

The United States military authorities would not cooperate

The whole Council came to the meeting

No one thought that there was anything more important to do or to attend. I bowed before them, and started giving my report.

Basically, it was a simple one, signifying that the United States military authorities, which were the greatest part of my contacts, would not cooperate.

I presented numerous reports, charts, lists, analyses, whatever I could do to validate my findings, but in the end, it boiled down to one thing.

The United States government, and the military in particular, were more afraid of the Grays than of the Anunnaki. Officials and military from other countries, such as England, Russia, and China, with whom I had also spoken, were no better. The fact that I had promised the officials that the Anunnaki would return, and would destroy them if they continued to associate with the Grays, frightened them a great deal.

But they argued that no matter how you look at it, the Anunnaki have been away, physically, for thousands of years. Their contacts and connections with the humans were not numerous, and they obviously did not care much.

*** *** ***

The Grays have been on earth for these same thousands of years, and their technology was advanced enough to annihilate the earth just as much as that of the Anunnaki, and they were more likely to act violently because their habitat, their experiments, and that their hopes would be threatened.

The results were that I could not persuade any government to disassociate from the Grays, or to trust me. At the end of my report I bowed, and sat down again, rather exhausted. All I wanted was to go home, sit under my favorite tree, have a cat or two lean against me, and wait for Marduchk to come home and tell me things were not so bad. But this was not to be.

The Council members deliberated without opening their Conduit to me, which was fine with me since I felt almost dissociated from it all. But after a short time, they opened it for our conversation.

"You have done well, Sinhar Ambar Anati," they communicated telepathically. "We now know where we stand, and we have made our final decision – we will go back to earth and cleanse it. Humanity is so utterly contaminated, only drastic measures can apply."

"How will you do that?" I asked. Cleanse an entire planet? Just like that? It seemed like a hopeless task, even for the Anunnaki. "Please explain to me, I am not sure I understand your plan."

"Very well," said the Council. "But we will need to go back a little. The point you must understand is, why did the Anunnaki originally come to earth? You know some of the reasons, but it wouldn't hurt to put everything in perspective for you."

"Yes, please do," I said. My fatigue had faded away completely, and I was eager to hear the details.

"Well, the Anunnaki did more than just come to earth. They have created it, million of years ago.

At that time, a group of Anunnaki scientists on Nibiru, including Sinhar Inanna, Sinhar Enki, Sinhar Ninlil, and others, had decided to extend their experiments in creating biological, living forms.

To do that, they needed a good plan and permission from the Council, so they worked it out and requested a meeting. The Council considered their suggestions, and agreed that such work would greatly increase Anunnaki knowledge and therefore would be an excellent idea to pursue.

However, they had one condition. The scientists were welcome to start working – but their laboratory would have to be off-planet.

The Council suspected that the introduction of new life forms, even in the isolated conditions of a laboratory, might be a threat to everyone already on Nibiru.

Large and small animals, and particularly people, even if they were to be created in the image of the Anunnaki, could not be tolerated to wander freely on Ashtari (Nibiru).

*** *** ***

The Anunnaki needed a planet-sized laboratory

The scientists devoted more thought to their project, and agreed that what they really needed was a planet-sized laboratory, where the creations could interact in a controlled environment without the interference of previously existing life forms.

The solution, to which the Council readily agreed, was to create a planet specifically for that purpose, at considerable distance from Nibiru, just in case.

And so the scientists went to the edge of the galaxy, and caused a star to explode and create a solar system.

The sun, which they named Shemesh (Sol) was surrounded by a few planets, and after a suitable amount of time (eons to humans, but nothing to the Anunnaki who can play with time as they wish) the Anunnaki went there to decide which planet would be the most appropriate.

For a short time they considered the planet humans call Mars, which at that time had plenty of water (the most important ingredient necessary for the laboratory, after oxygen) but finally settled on choosing Earth.

*** *** ***

The Anunnaki fostered the evolutionary process

They went to earth, started creating life forms, fostered the evolutionary process, and managed to accumulate an enormous amount of useful knowledge, all of which they telepathically transferred to Nibiru (Ashtari), where it was much appreciated. Unfortunately, the knowledge leaked to the Grays at Zeta Reticuli, and they decided to use humans, and sometimes cattle also, in their doomed experiments that were geared to save their own miserable race.

While doing this, they sadly contaminated the pure genetic material the Anunnaki scientists so painstakingly created, and the humans that resulted were no longer suitable for the study.

That was the reason why the Anunnaki deserted their research on earth.

"But you have never completely deserted humans," I said.

"No, not completely. We kept our connection. But the Grays really dug in, made their bases, lived underwater, and we had to keep away. And Grays' DNA have created greed, violence, and unbelievable cruelty within human nature.

Such characteristics were not part of the original DNA we used to create the humans. We had intended to create the humans in our image. Right now, we will assume, based on your research, that humanity is divided into three groups, regarding their level of contamination."

"Yes," I said, musing. "I have noticed the same thing. There are levels of contamination that make for various behaviour patterns. Actually, I have a lot of charts about it."

"Indeed," said the Council. "And excellent charts they are, and they gave us the structure.

*** *** ***

Humanity is divided into three groups, regarding their level of contamination

The first group:

The first group is those who exhibit heavy Grays' DNA contamination. They include:
- Those who torture or support torture by others, for any purpose whatsoever.
- Murderers (unless in self defense, which sometimes occurs in situations such as domestic abuse by a contaminated spouse).
- Rapists.
- Child molesters.
- Child abusers.
- Senior citizen abusers.
- Spouse abusers.
- Those who commit violent robberies.
- Illicit drug manufacturers, distributors and pushers.
- Those who engage in enslaving women, girls and young boys in prostitution rings.
- Criminals who use their form of religion as an excuse for their heinous crimes; this includes all religious fanaticsand extremists, such as suicide bombers.
- Those who destroy lives by depriving them of ways to support themselves, for their own greed.
- This includes the top echelon of corporate executives, who have lost any sense of humanity in their treatment of thousands of people and feel that this is "strictly business".
- Elected officials who have sold out for power and greed, and who are willing to destroy their own countries to aggrandize themselves.
- Elected officials who are willingly participating in destroying the ecology of the planet because of their close association with oil corporations, and other forms of commercial energy producing countries and their corrupt rulers.

- Any politician, military personnel, or anyone else who is engaging in trade with the Grays, allowing them to continue the atrocities in exchange for technical and military knowledge.
- Lawyers and judges who play games at the legal system for their own gain, sending child molesters, murderers, and other violent offenders back into society, ready to prey again on the innocent, all in the name of "reasonable doubt".
- Those who destroy lives and reputations by "identity theft".
- Those who torment animals.
- These include not only people who hurt and mutilate animals for their own sick pleasure, but also those who support dog fights, cockfights and bullfights, those who beat their horses, donkeys, or dogs, those who "legally" mutilate cats by removing their claws or hurting their vocal cords, owners of puppy mills who force female dogs to reproduce by "animal rape," and those who abandon their animals, or chain them indefinitely, sometimes allowing them to die by such neglect."
  - Prostitutes.

"Extremely dangerous people," I said. "I don't believe there is much chance of reforming them."

"None whatsoever," said the Council. "People who engage in such practices are doomed, as far as we are concerned. They are pure evil.

*** *** ***

The second group:

Anyway, here comes the second group, people who exhibit a medium level of Grays' DNA contamination.
These would include:

- People who believe that discipline requires physical punishment (in children or adults).
- Middle echelon executives who "only take orders" from their superiors as their corporations are destroying the economy of their own countries to save their own skin.
- Those, who in the name of fashion and beauty, have hurt countless young girls who have succumbed to eating disorders, some of whom have actually died, while the owners and designers made a fortune for themselves.
- Irresponsible parents who allow their children to grow up with Grays' values rather than human and Anunnaki values.
- Hunters of animals who kill only for food but do not feel a joy in killing and do not mutilate or torment the animals.
- Owners of "factory farms" whose animals are not deliberately tormented, but live a miserable life.
- People who eat any form of meat, since we believe in a strict vegetarian diet, supplemented by milk and eggs from animals that are treated humanely, and are allowed to live out their lives comfortably and die naturally".

"They may have some chance, I suppose" I said.
"Not much. Still, we hope they will try to work on their own redemption. We offer no guarantee, of course.

*** *** ***

The third group:

Then, there is the third group, people who exhibit light Grays' DNA contamination, and they include:
- People who are willing to advertise products that may be harmful, for gain.
- People who are willing to import products that may be harmful, for gain.

- People who object to social reform that may help the greater number of others, such as health care or better equalization of income, for gain.
- People who are engaged in the fur trade.
- People who are willing to influence others through brainwash-style advertising, such as the cosmetic industry, for gain.
- Racists, sexists, and ageists, who are willing to allow their prejudices to influence their behaviour to others.
- People who are willing to spend millions of dollars on frivolous pursuits, such as diamond studded collars for dogs, who don't really care about anything but love and food, or $200,000 cakes for a party, while millions around them are starving.
- People actively engaged in aggressive corporate take-overs, thus destroying the livelihoods of many.
- Anyone deliberately sending a computer virus for "fun and games" and thus destroying other people's livelihood and property.

*** *** ***

A Cataclysmic Event

The Anunnaki's Bubble

"I assume," I said, "that this is just a partial list. I can understand that. But what are your plans? What will you do with the people? With the animals?"

"We will plan a cataclysmic event, the likes of which can hardly be imagined by humans. As we told you, we have done it before, many times.

Other races have destroyed some of our experiments, and sometimes only a drastic cleansing would help. We will show you one soon, a cleansing that happened a few hundred years ago on a humanoid civilization much like the humans, but first, let us explain what will happen.

We will bring a bubble of a special substance, resembling anti-matter, but is not destructive, and cause it to touch the earth's atmosphere.

The bubble will be exactly the same size of planet Earth.

As soon as the two globes touch, all the humans that have been lucky enough not to be contaminated by Grays' DNA, and all the animals, plants, and those inanimate material which the Anunnaki wish to preserve (such as beautiful and historic monuments, art-filled museums, and great libraries, in addition to the homes of those saved) will be stripped from earth and absorbed into the bubble.

The fish, and other animals who need water, will be taken to an artificial ocean within the bubble. The birds will have plenty of places to perch on.

Nothing will be hurt or damaged – the humans and animals will feel nothing – they will be secure and comfortable within the bubble.

It is unlikely that they will even retain a clear memory of the event, because we would not wish them to be traumatized.

Then, the earth will be cleansed of all the pollution. For lack of a better description, try to imagine a huge vacuum cleaner removing all the landfills, eliminating all plastics, all the dirt, all the smog from the air, and all the filth from the ocean.

In a few short minutes, the earth will be sparkling clean, a pristine planet, the way it was when we had first created it.

Disposing of the garbage involves very high technology which humans simply do not as yet understand. The beautiful clean planet will be ready to be repopulated, and in an instant, the humans, animals, plants, and inanimate objects that were saved in the bubble, would be returned to earth.

*** *** ***

Anunnaki guides will be there for the humans

Anunnaki guides will be there for the humans, who would naturally need quite a bit of help to adjust to the new life."

"But those are only the uncontaminated ones," I said. "What about the others? How will they meet their fate?"

"Those who were heavily contaminated, and who were engaged in cruelty, greed, and violence for their own gain, will have no chance at all. They will simply be destroyed, and there is no need to even think about them any further. What is left are those who are of medium-level contamination, and the lighter level.

These groups will receive a warning to mend their lives, now, fourteen years before the event of 2022. When the event occurs, some of the people of light level contamination would have completely cleansed themselves through their efforts, and therefore would have been transferred, as clean beings, into the bubble. Others would have remained lightly contaminated.

Those of medium level contamination, who obviously require more work, would be divided into those who had succeeded in the cleansing, and had brought themselves into a light level contamination.

Those who remain at medium level, who did not do the work of cleansing properly, will be destroyed with the heavily contaminated ones.

All that will remain now would be the group of light contamination level, and if they wish to save themselves, they must go through Ba'abs, or Star Gates, into other dimensions, so that they could be evaluated by the Anunnaki.

If they can be cleansed, they go back to earth.

If not, they will live out their lives in another dimension, where conditions are much like our own earth before the cleansing. They will lead a normal life, but will not be able to reproduce, so eventually they will die out.

As for those who would succeed passing through the Ba'abs, the procedure is extremely difficult.

*** *** ***

Ba'abs (Star Gates) exist everywhere

Ba'abs (Star Gates) exist everywhere.

They are huge, magnificent Ba'abs that are used regularly by the Anunnaki to cross from one dimension to another. But there are also small ones, located in the street, in a tree, in an apartment building, in private homes, you name it.

They will become visible when the bubble touches with the earth, and those who were not taken into the bubble, or were not destroyed, must find their way into a Ba'ab. All Ba'abs look the same – they are a circle of shifting light of rainbow colors, very clearly defined.

People wishing to enter a Ba'ab must hurl themselves against it, and it will open and absorb any number of travelers.

As soon as you enter the Ba'ab, you are already in another dimension.

It is extremely frightening, a deep blackness illuminated by explosions, thunderbolts, and streaking comets. There is a very high level of a stormy, whoosh-like sound – the noise can be deafening – and the traveler is swept with violent speed forward, unable to resist or help the move, and constantly twirled and twisted in one direction, and then the other.

The traveler will feel dizzy, disoriented, and scared, and this lasts for an indefinite period of time. When this part is over, the traveler is thrown by a huge gust of wind into a tunnel, which is so brightly lit by blinding orange, yellow, and white light, that it is impossible to keep one's eyes open for more than a few seconds at a time.

The traveler hears horrible shrieks, screams, and howling of wind, and when the eyes are open, he or she sees bizarre faces, weird creatures, and unknown vehicles which always seem almost on the verge of colliding with the traveler, but somehow never do.

After a while, the traveler is thrown out of the tunnel onto solid ground, which may be quite painful but not permanently harmful. The light becomes normal and the sounds stop."

"Does that mean they have arrived safely?"

"Yes, at that point, the travelers have reached their destination. It looks much like earth, but it is devoid of people or animals, and plants and houses look very dim, as if the travelers found themselves in virtual reality.

Then, the traveler begins to see people materialize against the cardboard-like background.

This takes time, the images of people float as if from thin air, but then, all of a sudden, reality shifts and the travelers find themselves in a real world.

Animals, incidentally, will never materialize. All of them have been returned to earth, to their proper places, as mentioned before. They are not needed here, since no animal labor or the eating of animals is permitted by the Anunnaki, who abhor such practices.

From then on, the travelers will eat only a vegetarian diet. In this dimension, the travelers will meet a few Anunnaki, who will direct them to their evaluation and possible cleansing.

Only those who make it would be returned to earth. Those who cannot be cleansed will be sent, through a Ba'ab, to the dimension we have mentioned before, where they will live out their lives, but will not be able reproduce.

The Anunnaki do not wish to kill them, since they are not inherently evil like the heavily contaminated ones. But they cannot let them reproduce the bad DNA; the Anunnaki do not indulge in sentimental pity, and are fully aware that any form of evil should not be allowed to exist."

"The treatment of the humans is extreme," I said calmly, "but not unjust. They have brought it upon themselves since they would not listen to the warning."

"Well said, Sinhar Ambar Anati," said the Council. "Spoken like a true Anunnaki."

"You said you would show me how this is done," I said. "I do wonder how the earth would be cleansed."

"Yes," said the Council. "Look at the Miraya." Naturally, there was a huge Miraya on one of the walls, and I waited while the Council made preparations for the visions to appear.

"It will be emotionally harrowing to watch that, Sinhar Ambar Anati," said one of the Council. "Are you sure you want to see it?"

"Yes," I said. "I think I should. Perhaps there is still something I can do."

"I think there is," said the Council, and at this point a small light appeared in the Miraya. The light grew, and I suddenly saw a bubble, looking much like a simple soap bubble, on the screen.

It started to travel, and in a very short time I saw it approach the unmistakable shape and color of earth. The two globes touched, and I saw streams of light emanating from the earth and disappearing into the bubble.

"In these streams of light, all the clean people, all the animals, and all the inanimate objects we have chosen are transferred to the bubble for safe keeping," said the Council. "Also, the Ba'abs are opening for those who might try to escape into them. We will now zoom in closer and show you the cleansing itself."

The Miraya showed a growing image, and after a few minutes I saw a terrain which I did not recognize, but it seemed earth-like.

The people were ape-like humanoids, but obviously they bore a very close resemblance to humanity. They even wore similar clothes.

The area looked devastated – after all, the houses the people had lived in, any animal they may have had, all the plants, and many buildings, had already disappeared into the bubble.

So the environment was totally alien and frightening to these people. They looked disoriented, staring at the sky, running around, searching for missing people. The whole scene was of one of terrible confusion.

The sun seemed to undergo an eclipse, but it was not a natural one. A massive ceiling of metal shapes of machinery, gadgets, wheels, and shifting lights covered the sky.

They were ominously silent, as if waiting. I imagined that looking at them from below was immensely frightening.

The people seemed to have lost their minds, they were running around in circles, some stampeded and trampled each other. I saw people running into churches and heard the bells toll.

Naturally, religious leaders would not be saved, or go through the Ba'abs, but still tried to call their congregations in, hoping for some miracle.

Everywhere I saw Ba'abs, those colorful circles, and people smashing themselves into them in an attempt to escape.
Some went through.
Others were thrown back. The Ba'abs could determine the level of contamination and only allow the righteous ones to pass through, hurling the others back at some distance.
"Total chaos," I said.
"It's even worse than you can imagine," said the Council. "In various cities, people tried to reach their governments, without much success.

The only officials that have stayed at their posts, issued orders to avoid any interference with the extraterrestrials, since it would make everything even more dangerous and no one on the planet we are showing you had the technology to match.
The officials' orders were ignored, particularly by those in rural areas, who were used to self sufficiency. These people confronted the Anunnaki, started shooting at them with their guns.
As in other areas, which of course had many good people living in them, only the violent ones have remained, since the others have already escaped.
Acting stupidly, they annoyed the Anunnaki with their inept shooting until the Anunnaki decided to paralyze them with special beams of light, for a limited time.

***   ***   ***

The Final Stage

When the beams effects wore off, some resumed their doomed attempts to fight, and at this point the Anunnaki started the final stage."

"Let me see the final stage," I said.

From the bottom of the spaceships, a special substance was diffused, and it landed in huge, swirling streams. It was a black liquid, mixed with light and electricity, and some strange sparkling particles, which I was sure was a form of energy or radiation.

"It smells like fire and brimstone, but strangely, it is cold to the touch. Yet, it burns everything that touches it. This is a tool of annihilation, a tool that no one can fight," said the Council. I looked on, without comment.

The substance slithered inexorably over the ground, the buildings, and the stranded cars like icy cold lava waves. It swept away many people, killing them instantly.

Once it covered a large area, it began to coagulate, and as it did so, it expanded and rose up, foot by foot, until it reached the height of an eight storied building. Slowly, it seemed to harden, solidifying itself into steel-like state.

Huge stacks of smoke rose up into the sky, cars melted, buildings collapsed, and fires started everywhere, seemingly not only by the touch of the substance, but spontaneously, when the wind carries the particles of energy into flammable materials. The combination of images and sounds was that of chaos, pain, confusion, and death.

I imagined that the fire and brimstone smell had now mixed with that of burning flesh and of melting metal, plastic and rubber.

Then, all of a sudden, the substance stopped growing, and assumed the appearance of craggy mountains, with sharp edges and canyons. A very few who had survived, but had nowhere to go to, now tried to climb on the substance, since the earth itself was buried in it. This was futile, since the substance was too slippery for the climb. They started to fall and slip, and were instantly killed.

"These conditions will continue over the entire world for two days; no one will be left alive on the scorched earth," said the Council. I remained silent. "Let us move the scene into the fourth day," said the Council. "You see, at that point, which must have been the third day, all the spaceships left, and in twenty-four hours, the substance and all it consumed turned to dust. The earth became ready for the vast cleansing."

Other spaceships appear on the screen, of completely different appearance. The new ones were not be circular like the others, but crescent shaped, and of pleasant colors, nothing frightening about them.

They activated the huge vacuum system, and an enormous cloud of black dust came up in swirling, filthy streams. It did not take long; in a few minutes the whole cloud was sucked into the machines, and the earth was ready for new life.

With so much death and destruction, a small part of me wanted to pray for the souls of the ones who were killed.

Something in my head wanted to turn to God. Then I laughed. If our kind of paternal God had existed, He would have not allowed humans to be so cruel, so horrible, as to cause a need for such a massive cleansing.

I was beginning to grasp the nature of All-That-Is, the concept of a creative God that encompassed everything and learned from it voraciously. He, she or it would not have mercy on our souls. I bowed my head, and then raised it and looked at the Council.

"I see the need," I said. "I would like to request one more trip, one more attempt to convince the officials about this cleansing, let them warn the earth. If I fail, my blessing goes with your cleansing. The evil must be removed."

"We are proud of you, Sinhar Ambar Anati," said Sinhar Inannaschamra verbally. "High Council, I have told you that, years ago. She is a true Anunnaki."

"Indeed she is, Sinhar Inannaschamra. Indeed she is, and she has our permission to go for the final attempt," said the Council. "We shall have a plan soon." Then they bowed and left.

As usual, Sinhar Inannaschamra stayed with me, and we walked home together.

"So the earth will be cleansed," I said.

"The contaminated DNA will be removed. So far, so good. But what is going to happen afterwards? I imagine the world will be considerably changed."

"You won't recognize be able to it," said Sinhar Inannaschamra. "It will be vastly improved, believe me. The first thing to disappear is the root of all evil – money."

"Really? Money will no longer exist?"

"Think about it, Victoria. Would the Anunnaki support any of humanity's greed-infested systems? The most profound change will be the abolition of money and every system that is attached to money.

People will work in their chosen professions, or a new profession that they will adopt, and produce or serve as usual."

"But how will they survive?

How will they get food, lodging and clothes? In other words, if they don't have money, how will they be paid?"

"They will not be paid, but they will have everything that they need, just like we do on Nibiru. Everyone will have a comfortable home, designed to his or her taste.

Good food for them and for their pets, beautiful clothes, nice jewelry, cosmetics, diapers for babies, toys, hobby supplies, etc. will always be available in huge cooperatives that will look like excellent supermarkets, open day and night so that no one will ever lack for anything.

What everyone considers luxury items will also be available – the Anunnaki have no desire to have humans live in austerity.

Humans will always have books, TV, radio, home movies, classic films etc. They can go to the theater, the ballet, the symphony orchestra, chamber music performances, movie theaters and always for free. The only thing the Anunnaki will deprive humans of is excess.

There will be no need for hoarding, since everything will always be available, and no one will be able to be richer than their neighbors. Equality will be established, and appreciated by those who are not contaminated by the greed and meanness of the Grays.

"So what about places like Fort Knox?"

"No need for such places anymore. Ford Knox is going to be destroyed, and the gold used for ornamental purposes. That is the only reason people will value gold now – its beauty. A good artist can create some pretty good pieces from such a lovely substance, which will be widely available after the great change.

The same will happen, incidentally, with diamonds, and other gems. Their intrinsic value will disappear, so jewelry will only be appreciated for its intricate and elegant design, not for how many carats a stone weighs.

Because of that, there will be no need for the IRS, the Social Security system, and other such organizations. The elimination of the money system will cause many professions to disappear, such as accountants, bankers, tax preparers, security guards, and IRS employees."

"Any other changes?"

"Of course. Money will not be the only 'victim.'

In a society that consists of good people, people who have no need or desire to commit any crime whatsoever, there will be no need for the legal system.

All organizations pertaining to the law and law enforcement will disappear, including the Supreme Court. And of course, there will be no prisons. This will eliminate many professions as well, such as lawyers, judges, court clerks, prison officials, police officers and guards."

"You know, Sinhar Inannaschamra, this sounds like a lovely place to live in."

"Built in the image of Nibiru, of course. All governments will be abolished. No elected officials, no presidents, no kings. People who are good do not need anyone telling them how to live, they do it instinctively. This will eliminate thousands of positions, such as presidents, kings, governors, mayors, all government employees, social workers, and child protection agencies.

And don't forget that since the Anunnaki technology is going to keep humans healthy, there will be no need for hospitals or clinics, other than those devoted to childbirth, and much of the work there will be done without the need for people.

In addition, there will not be any incidents of insanity or mania or depression.

This will eliminate the positions of most doctors and nurses, and of additional employees such as hospital administration, hospital billing, psychiatrists, psychologists, and hospital janitors, to name a few."

"So no one will be sick, what a world," I said. "I can imagine that humans will no longer have the need for cars and airplanes, right?"

"Indeed. There will be advanced technology that will allow for much more efficient forms of transportation and the use of clean and efficient energy, and in the process, we will eliminate the need for any fossil fuels.

This will remove more professions from the list, such as gas stations, agencies supplying us with electricity and gas, car manufacturers, airplane manufacturers, and highway builders."

"It will be hard to adjust to such living."

"I am not sure about that. Remember, the only people remaining are not contaminated.

They don't need or want wealth, really preferring to be happy, creative, comfortable and spiritually fulfilled. There will be even more changes. Some miscellaneous professions will not remain, since they will no longer be appreciated or needed.

For example, the fashion industry, with its cruel attempts to make women into slaves of someone else's ideas of beauty, will entirely disappear.

Beautiful clothing will be created by individual designers or by anyone who likes to indulge in it as a creative hobby. Advertising, of course, will vanish as well.

So no one will need runway models, beauty contest organizers, manicurists, cosmetologists, or advertising commercials actors and voice over artists."

"So what will happen to the clean people who worked in these professions?" I asked, envisioning a mass of unemployed, confused people.

"Nothing to be alarmed about. Those who will lose their professions will be trained for another profession, always entirely of their own choice, that will give them pleasure and pride to pursue.

Even those who have not lost their profession, but who feel the need for a change, will be encouraged to pursue a career change. As a matter of fact, since the life expectancy of each and every person will be greatly increased, it is expected that many people will have numerous career changes as time goes by.

Life-long study is always encouraged by the Anunnaki, who consider the acquisition of knowledge the most enjoyable thing a person can do."

"From what you say, many professions that are very well respected today, mostly because they are highly paid, will disappear. I wonder if such individuals will be able to adjust."

"They usually do. Remember, many professions will change in the way they are perceived.

For example, the teaching profession, for both children and adults, will become the most highly respected profession in the world. Librarians will be very highly regarded.

Gardeners will be of great importance. Historians and writers will be greatly valued.

But of course, in a world that judges a person by what he or she is, not by how much money is accumulated, every profession will be appreciated for its usefulness to the entire community. So I think the great majority of people will be pleased with our changes."

"Only the survivors…"

"True," said Sinhar Inannaschamra casually.

"The population will be greatly decreased, of course." We entered my home in silence, and I materialized some coffee and fruit for us in a dream state.

I found it hard to believe that I, of all people, had contributed one of the major reasons to the end of the world as we know it. I always used to think it would be accomplished by fanatics or by governments that supported nuclear explosions. Well, one lives and learns.

*** *** ***

The Final Clash

How I went to earth to make one final attempt to convince the humans to give up their affiliations with the Grays. How the humans tried to betray my trust, and the explosive results that would bring not only extreme danger to myself, but the return of the Anunnaki in 2022.

One last time, I said to myself. This is their only chance. If they agreed to accept the final option to change their ways, good. If not, I would not stand in the way of the Council's plan of cleansing the earth.

It would hurt me a great deal to think of the billions that were about to die. But there would be no more opposition on my part. I would obey the Council, no matter how badly I would feel.

With the weariness of an act that was performed hundreds of times over in the past seventeen years, I contacted the highest level military personnel at an important air base which I will call North X, since of course, I cannot reveal it's real name. As always, they had no choice but to meet with me.

At this time, anyway, after all these years of negotiations with everyone, including some presidents of the United States and Europe, I was pretty well known – and highly disliked. Perhaps I was even a little feared.

The individual I spoke to was very agreeable, and proceeded to arrange the details for the meeting with me. "By the way," I said, after all was decided upon. "If a single shape-shifting Gray will be at the meeting, I will leave immediately. And believe me, I always recognize a shape-shifter. You see, this is the last meeting I plan to have with any human, and the presence of a Gray will defeat the purpose of it."

"There will be no Grays at the meeting, Ms. Anati," said my contact. "I can promise you that.

My colleagues and I have already discussed the issue before you and I came to arrange the meeting.

They feel the same way as you do." Well, that was a good sign, I thought. We shall see.

Arriving at the air base, I was immediately taken to a small, ordinary conference room. A few people rose from their seats at the conference table as I came in.

There were two generals in military uniform, one a retired admiral, who worked for the NSA as a consultant, and was a co-proprietor of a major civilian jet propulsion company, a colonel who had worked as test pilot for the Mcdonnell Douglas and Boeing companies, and a person that I guessed represented the White House.

As always, they were extremely polite, and indeed, none of them was a Gray. Perhaps by that time, they finally believed that I could recognize a shape-shifter, or perhaps they had their own agenda. I think, in light of what took place later, that the second option was the correct one. They wanted to hide the meeting from the Grays.

We sat around the table, and they turned to me, ready to hear my offer. They thought that I still was ready to negotiate. Of course, the time for negotiations was over, but they did not realize that.

"Allow me to summarize the current situation for you, gentlemen, I said. "Whether you take action now or later, you will be facing an extraterrestrial threat. The threat you have now, comes from the Grays who are controlling your science and space program, and are dominating a major part of the earth.

The Grays know that you have tried, for many years, to find a weapon system to counter attack them. And they know very well that you have started this program when President Reagan took office. They also know that you failed to develop such a weapon system on your own.

That means that you are defenseless. You know it, and they are aware of it. This is why you allow the Grays to go on with the atrocities and the abductions of human beings. It makes you feel safer around them. However, what you don't understand is that the Grays will not be satisfied by only kidnapping people and going on with their abominable experiments.

All their experiments are aimed at saving their own doomed race, which is slowly dying from an epidemic of Progeria which they cannot control. By and large, they have failed. So now they want permanent visible bases on the surface of the earth, and much bigger scope for further experiments on a larger scale."

"They have never mentioned this plan to us," said the White House representative.

"Of course not. This is top secret. They know you will feel like cornered rats and fight back."

"So what will happen when they take over?" asked the Admiral.

"They will kill many humans. The rest will be put in concentration camps, to be available for use whenever needed. In other words, you will be taken over, and this, to all intents and purposes, will be the end of the human race."

"I see," answered the Admiral, in a low voice. He was clearly thoughtful.

"What is the later threat you have mentioned?" asked one of the generals.

"It will come from the Anunnaki. You don't feel it now, not quite yet, but it is just as real. However, it is very different from the threat of the Grays.

The Anunnaki are not interested in establishing any bases on the surface of the earth or in the oceans, nor do they wish to experiment on you.

They want, quite simply, the complete destruction of your military systems, submarines, aircraft carriers, and spy satellites. They will throw an electro-plasmic shield over the earth, which will prevent airplanes from taking off.

This will apply to every airplane, no matter how big or small, military, commercial, or private. Gravity will become twelve hundred times stronger than it is now, preventing everything on earth from moving, including human beings.

Then, a kind of artificial lava will finish off the biosystem of the earth. You will not be able to fight it, for the simple reason that you do not know what it is made off.

In addition, the Anunnaki will bring on huge tsunamis. However, the worst part will be the issue of magnetism. Positive and negative magnetism will be distorted, and this will alter the laws of physics on earth.

This scenario may sound like science fiction, but you know better than that. It will start around the end of 2021. You will suddenly be confronted by confusion, when all clocks and watches will stop, and ships at sea will collide with each other without knowing the reason, among other results of the changed polar magnetism."

"We would consider severing all relations with the Grays," said the representative of the White House. "That is, on one condition."

"I don't think the Anunnaki will be willing to negotiate conditions," I said, "but do tell me anyway. Perhaps something can be done."

"If the Anunnaki will send an official military delegation from Nibiru right away, bringing with them scientists to develop a system like the plasmic belt and the Star Wars program, and guarantee to us that the United States can have complete military control over the earth, we will be willing to cooperate with them. Also, we want a system that will allow us to cause major ecological catastrophes to North Korea, Iran, China, Afghanistan, and parts of Russia. Of course it should look like a natural catastrophe, not anything man-made," said the White House representative.

"The Anunnaki will not give you any such programs," I said resolutely. "It is not at all within their plans."

"So you are refusing to protect us! If you don't protect us, why should we break our agreement with the Grays? After all, how do we know you are really coming back, or even if you are telling the truth about the Grays' plans? And quite frankly, why such a sudden interest in human affairs on the part of the Anunnaki, and in Americans in particular?

"Nonsense," I said. "They are not particularly interested in the Americans, you are not more important than anyone else on earth. The only reason for contacting you in particular is the fact that the Grays have their bases in America.

All the star gates, the genetic laboratory facilities and installations are either underground in America or in the American military bases. In short, the Grays are contaminating human DNA from right here."

I could see that they believed me. But they were still naïve enough to believe that the Grays will eventually help them develop the Star Weapon system they have promised but failed to deliver. The Americans still wanted to buy some time, and they were not really sure how to do that. I could feel their confusion.

"Ms. Anati," said the Admiral. "We would like a little time to confer before giving you our final answer. If you don't mind, allow me to escort you to one of our private guest lounges. They are quite comfortable, I'll arrange for coffee and some refreshments, and we will come back for you in an hour to finalize our plan. Would that be all right?"

It would have been just fine, had this been the real plan. Very natural and appropriate. But my Conduit was open all along, and I read their thoughts freely.

I knew what they meant to do to me, and it did not include coffee or refreshments, nor did it take place in a guest lounge. But I decided to play their game, and went quietly with the Admiral, who chatted pleasantly while escorting me to an elevator.

The ride on the elevator was long. Very long. We went down, obviously into some underground facility. I said nothing about it and pretended all was well. Eventually, the elevator stopped, the door opened, and at the door, three or four soldiers waited for me.

I was grabbed unceremoniously, while the Admiral went back into the elevator, not even giving me a glance. I was shoved into a cell, they locked the door behind me, and I was left alone in their underground prison.

As I said, I knew this was coming, but having my resources, I had no reason to fear these people. I could, of course, dematerialize myself and get out any time I wanted.

So I sat on the narrow bed, directed my Conduit, and listened to their conversation.

I must admit that I experienced a slight feeling of claustrophobia. I have come so close to being an extraterrestrial that it was inevitable.

But I repressed it, reminded myself that I could leave any time I wanted, and listened carefully to the conversation in the conference room.

"It won't take long, they are all terribly claustrophobic," said the Admiral. "Her energy will drain away, like a battery, very soon."

"Will she die?" asked the White House representative anxiously. "I am not sure this is a good strategy, we may be held accountable for any issues that may arise from her arrest."

"She won't die so quickly. She will go insane first," said the Admiral.

"Well, so what do we do now?" asked the retired pilot.

"We have all sort of options, but what is clear to me is that we must confuse the Anunnaki and get them off our trail," said one of the generals.

"But she may contact the Anunnaki first," said the other general.

"This will be a good thing," said the Admiral. "At the same time she contacts them, we will send signals that will confuse them. They won't be able to decide where to go to get her. In the meantime, she will go mad."

"Are you sure they drain away like the Grays?" asked the first general.

"Oh, yes, they are all the same, these filthy aliens," said the Admiral. "Let her rot here, and we will have the Anunnaki and the Grays so confused, they will fight each other, and that will take care of all our problems."

At this moment, something happened in my own mind. I realized that I no longer wanted to save these people. They were pure evil, and the Anunnaki do not tolerate evil.

I felt, to my own amazement, that I no longer cared about how many contaminated humans would die in the cleansing. I knew the Anunnaki will save the clean ones. Let the others go. I grinned.

Yes, I had finally started thinking like a full Anunnaki. What's more, I felt that I was quite capable of killing them myself.

I remembered how shocked I was when my dear, kind, loving husband Marduchk had killed without batting an eyelash. I was even more shocked when my beloved sister-in-law told me that she had killed too, on various missions she had undertaken. Now I understood.

I was not angry with these treacherous creatures. A cold, determined feeling went through my mind instead. It was all so simple. They were evil, and so they had to die.

Calmly, I created a plasmic shield around me. Nothing in the known universe could penetrate it. Wearing it, I could pass through an exploding star and survive.

Then, I made some calculations, figuring out how much energy was needed to blow up the entire base, killing everyone inside it in an instant. The plasmic shield was invisible and I could hear perfectly well through it until I chose to switch the audio off.

I materialized myself back into the conference room. The look on their faces when they saw me was so priceless, I had to laugh.

"Well, gentlemen," I said quite politely, "this is the end. I could have exploded the air base from anywhere on the face of the earth, but I wanted to give you the news myself."

They must have communicated quickly with some of the personnel, because about fifteen soldiers, well-armed with all sorts of paraphernalia, burst into the room and rushed to grab me.

The plasmic shield made them fly backwards, and some hit the wall. One or two fainted from the blow.

"I would not bother, if I were you, gentlemen," I said. "Believe me, there is absolutely nothing you can do. Well, it's time to blow up the air base, so good bye."

"Please, Ms. Anati, we will do what the Anunnaki ask us!" cried the White House representative. "Yes, yes, tell the Anunnaki we have no conditions! We will obey them implicitly!" said the Admiral. The others just stood there, terrorized.

A few years ago, perhaps I would have taken pity on them. I would have thought of their wives, their children and pets… by now I knew this was stupid sentimentality that made me less than an Anunnaki. That was over now.

"Too late, gentlemen," I said. "Good bye." I turned down the audio, and activated the explosion.

It looked like a nuclear bomb. It sounded like one, even through the plasmic shield. And it worked like one, too. Nothing was left of building; I was now standing alone in a huge, black, gaping hole in the ground.

From other buildings, people came out, screaming, running wildly. I ignored them, nodded with satisfaction at the cleanliness of the job, turned away, and proceeded to materialize myself in another continent.

I did not want CIA agents hunting and bothering me like flies and gnats. Of course, I could kill them. But what is the point of doing the Anunnaki cleansing job for them all by myself?

Well, it was time to leave earth. If I ever came back to it, after it was cleansed, I would no longer be the same woman. I have changed, and my place now was on Nibiru. However, I could not just call on Marduchk and ask him to pick me up as usual. Ahead of me was another task, the most important task of all.

This task would be dangerous, tremendously risky, but unavoidable, and I would have to do it alone. Somehow or other, I would have to leave everything of me that was human right here on earth. Only then would I be able to place my mind into the clean, perfect Anunnaki body that was prepared for me some years ago. I would have to do that with no traces of humanity, or of any possible contamination.

And for that, I would have to shed my old body like the skin of a snake, leave it on earth, and go home not in a space ship, but rather, send my mind through a multidimensional Ba'ab. Which meant, in human terms, that I would simply have to die."

*** *** ***

Coding and Decoding the Significance of the Year 2022

2022 is the year when the Anunnaki plan to come back to earth and cleanse it from the Grays' contamination. This year has great significance if it is coded in Hebrew.
There are two ways of interpretation.

First Interpretation of the Code

Take the number 2022 and translate it into the Hebrew alphabet. Remember that Hebrew is read from right to left, and follow the numbers in that sequence. This gives you the word:
2022=בבאב
2 is ב, the second letter of the Hebrew alpha-bet.
The 0 becomes א because:
0 = The Infinite = God = The One. The א is the first letter in the Hebrew Alphabet, namely, The One.
The word reads, phonetically, bb'ab, and it means ba-Ba'ab: In the Ba'ab.

Ba'ab means: Stargate of the Anunnaki.
From this stargate the Anunnaki spaceships enter and exit galaxies, skies, multiple universes, parallel dimensions and outer space.
Also from this Ba'ab, a person exits our physical world to enter the dimension (Universe) of extraterrestrials.

Interpretation and meaning: Once you enter the year 2022, you will automatically enter the Ba'ab of Liberation – but only if you are not contaminated, or if, starting right now, you attempt to cleanse yourself.

Second Interpretation of the Code

Add the numbers that appear in the year 2022.
2 + 0 + 2 + 2 = 6
According to the Ulema and the "Book of Rama-Dosh", the number 6 means: Liberation.

Interpretation and meaning:
The liberation from the contamination and control of the Grays.

Characteristics of the number 6

6 is a perfect number, also a "Triangular" number. It is the geometrical value of the word "Space" in Anak'h, the Anunnaki language, and "Spirit" in the Phoenician language. In the Greek oracles it is "Delta".

This geometrical form and its numerical value is also the "Logo" of the Anunnaki, because it represents the triangle. And inverted the triangle was shown on the uniforms of the American military personnel and scientists who work on the "Black Projects" and alien reverse engineering at secret bases, and genetic laboratories in the United States.

Many insiders and top echelon military men reported that they have seen the "Triangle"/"Delta" sign on several crashed UFOs stored in secret military bases.

*** *** ***

The number 6, Carbon and the Creation of Mankind

Worth mentioning here is that the chemical element carbon has an atomic number of 6. In the "Book of Rama-Dosh", the word "Carbon" was used to represent the source of life and was the first element used by the Anunnaki to genetically create the early human race. Everything is connected.

The Ulema who are the custodians of the Anunnaki "Book of Rama-Dosh" explain that the number "6" is the secret code of the year 2022. It is a vital number because it represents the 6 known directions known to mankind: directions: north, south, east, west, up and down.
In 2022, two more directions or dimensions will be added. And the human race in 2022, will understand the nature of these 2 additional dimensions which are not very far from the physical fourth dimension we live in.
The fifth dimension could be considered as a spatial trampoline, and the sixth dimension is the destination or rendezvous of the human race with the Anunnaki.

*** *** ***

The number 6 is one of the six major extraterrestrial hot spots on Earth

"6" as a pentagonal pyramidal number is explained in the Anunnaki's manuscript as one of the six major extraterrestrial hot spots on Earth. "6" is the Anti-Ba'ab.
The other five are: Baalbeck, Arwad, Tyre, Nippur, and Malta. Does this predict or hint to the landing areas of the Anunnaki when they return to earth in 2022?
Some psychics think so. It is an entertaining idea, but an unlikely scenario.

The sixth letter in the Phoenician Alphabet is "Waw". Once the corners of the letter "Waw" are joined in a stroke of a pen, it becomes a perfect triangle.
This was the "Unification" numerical code for the Anunnaki and early Phoenicians of Baalbeck and Tyre.
The Ulema (Seers, Sages and Men of Knowledge in Arabic) also used the Anunnaki-Phoenician letter "Waw" in their Arabic dialect. It is pronounced in the same way, and means exactly the very same thing: "With" or "With others".
In Phoenician, "Waw" means hook.

Statue of a Phoenician goddess found in Malta.

Ruins of ancient Malta, which is one of the six major extraterrestrial hot spots on Earth.

The ancient walls of Malta.

Ruins of Baalbeck, one of the earliest Anunnaki's cities/colonies on Earth.

The Trilithon of Baalbeck, part of the early space centers of the Anunnaki in the Near East.

Another view of the legendary Trilithon of Baalbeck.

Tomb of Hiram, King of Tyre, founder of the first Freemasonry Rite in the world, and an offspring of the remnants of the Anunnaki in the Near East.

Ruins of the ancient city of Tyre in Phoenicia (Modern day Lebanon). Tyre was one of the six major esoteric cities of the Anunnaki on Earth.

Tyre (Sour) today; a Shiite Muslim city in Southern Lebanon.

Staircase within the Ziggurat of Nippur. The ancient city of Nippur in Iraq, was one of the six major extraterrestrial hot spots on Earth.

A tower towards the heavens in Nippur.
Ur Nammu atop the Ziggurat (Tower of Babel) at Ur.

The Phoenician "Hook":
The esoteric and spiritual meaning of the hook is "Ascension", and "Liberation". It was constantly chanted in the secret rituals of the Phoenician gods Adoon (Adon, Adonis, Adonai) and Melkart.

*** *** ***

Meaning of the number 6 in Anunnaki-Phoenician Alphabets

The Phoenician "Hook" also meant a "Celestial Gate".
This is how we got the word "Ba'ab" meaning exactly the extraterrestrial stairway to heaven. "Waw" in the Phoenician Alphabet is in fact an Anunnaki symbol and written like a "Y".
The letter "Y" represents a base (Earth) and two additional dimensions on the right and on the left. These are the two additional dimensions beyond ours that the Anunnaki code reveals. It is not as complicated as you might think. It is only a secret and hidden message.
It corresponds to the Hebrew "Vav".

Two united "Vav" represent the "Ascension" and the two additional dimensions beyond the physical fourth dimension.
In Aramaic "Waw" is written and pronounced like the Phoenician and Anunnaki "Waw".

Facts:
Despite the US constant denial of any contact with aliens, many statements given by top American military scientists and a high-ranking Annunaki's personal revelations show without any doubt, that in fact:

1-While different alien races do live and work on planet earth, the Anunnaki do not.

2-The Grays who originally came from Zeta Reticuli have several bases and genetic laboratories, fully operational in the United States. The Anunnaki left our planet earth thousands of years ago.

3-The Grays have helped the military in developing advanced spatial weapons/missiles systems. The first test occurred in 1984, and the Russians became aware of these significant military tests around 1985.
The Anunnaki offered the United States advanced technology for scientific and humanitarian purposes, but the military wanted very advanced weapon systems instead. The Anunnaki refused.

4-The Grays kept on abducting humans for various reasons, and for a very long time, and the United States government allowed these abductions.
The Anunnaki are not in the abduction business.
Whether the Grays' abductions occurred with, or without the consent of our government remains irrelevant, because a treaty was signed between the US and 4 different alien races permitting such horrible acts.
In exchange for "closing their eyes" NASA, NSA, the CIA, the navy and the Air Force received very advanced extraterrestrial technology.
The Anunnaki never participated in these atrocities.

5-A very high level meeting between the United States and a representative of the High Council of the Anunnaki took place at the Four Seasons Hotel in Georgetown, Washington, D.C.

6-The United States refused to terminate their formal relationships with the Grays, and categorically rejected an offer submitted by an entity representing the Anunnaki.

7-The United States government did not believe that the Anunnaki had any vital interest in the human race, and especially the United States.

8-The United States were officially notified that the Anunnaki shall return to earth in 2022.
This notification was never taken seriously by those who attended the meeting in Washington, D.C., however scientists from MIT and top executives at a major corporation (military contractor) known for its jet propulsion projects and headed by a former high ranking military commander, wrote a memo and a summary of findings pertaining to the topics discussed during that infamous meeting, and submitted their memoranda to The White House.
Insiders leaked very disturbing information about a lethal clash between the Anunnaki official and military guards at a well-publicized military base known for its "black projects" and extraterrestrial technology-reverse engineering.

*** *** ***

In 1947, a Grays' spacecraft crashed in Roswell

In 1947, a Grays' spacecraft crashed in Roswell. Two Grays died from the impact, but one survived. The Americans held him underground at Andrews Air Force Base.
Strangely enough, a sort of friendship was developed between the Gray and two American civilian scientists, something that we still don't understand, but there it was.

At that time, the military and CIA were only interested in acquiring advanced military weapons systems, not in a friendship with an alien. But somehow they became friends.
The military kept everything under cover and did not even inform even Congress or the President of the United States.

One general actually said, 'Civilians and politicians come and go. But we, the military, that is our career.
Therefore, they should not be informed and if Congress will not be told, consequently the American public should not be told

either.' That was the policy that was adopted on a regular basis ever since."

*** *** ***

According to an Anunnaki record, and a revelation by Victoria (Ambar Anati, the Anunnaki official delegate) we have the following information:
Victoria talking to another Anunnaki: "That is frightening," I said. "The military should not control the decision."
"Indeed they should not. Look at the Miraya, Sinhar Ambar Anati.
Here is one of the first conversations between the surviving Gray and the two American scientists."

Statement by Ambar Anati on record

Statement by Ambar Anati on record: "On the screen, I saw an office, quite ordinary and simply furnished. Two men and a Gray sat around an empty desk. They seemed comfortable, there was no tension, as you might expect in such a company. Then, the sound came from the Miraya. (A monitor)
One of the American scientists,[1] asked the Gray:
-"So where did you come from? And why are you here?"
-"We have been here for thousands of years," said the Gray, in perfect English, though his voice had the usual scratchy sound of his race. "We have our bases underwater, in the Pacific, near Puerto Rico, and under Alaska's glaciers."
-"Thousands of years?"
-"That is so. We consider ourselves the first and the legitimate inhabitants and owners of the earth. You are not. We are here because we need natural resources that exist on earth and in the oceans."

---

[1] A note from Victoria: we cannot reveal the scientist's name, since this could endanger his family.

-"Seems to me this is not all you need, buddy," said the other scientist, grinning and lighting a cigarette.
-"This is true. We also need some live organisms, and various substances we can extract from human bodies."
-"And did you get all you want?" asked the first scientist.
-"Yes, by and large. We need them on a constant basis," said the Gray. "The natural resources of the earth and the water are regularly mined. The human substances are more difficult to obtain. We get them from the humans we abduct."

The two scientists nodded in agreement, totally unimpressed by the mention of the abductions.
They really did not seem to mind.
-"What bugs me," said the first scientist, "is that we tried so hard to reverse engineer your spaceship, ever since we got it after the crash in Roswell. We just can't do it. You have to help us decipher the codes on the screens we found inside the spaceship, and also the geometric and scientific symbols on the grids and measuring tapes we found scattered around the spaceship.
Our team is getting impatient; they may even threaten to kill you, you know. The two of us are friendly with you, but the team is getting ugly, and the boss is mad."
-"What is the point?" said the Gray without showing any emotion, not even fear regarding the threat. "Even if I teach you how things work, and decipher all the codes for you, you will not be able to reverse engineer our technology, because you don't have the raw materials. Look at this."

From somewhere around his body, he pulled out a piece of metal.
-"This is a very light metal yet stronger than any material known on earth. Yet this sheet of metal could float in the air, and can be bent and folded like paper and then, open up on its own. Look!" He demonstrated. The metal seemed to be indestructible.
-"You must understand that we are willing to reveal plenty of information," said the Gray. "But we can only do so if you will

allow me to go home. I need to recharge my body, it's like a battery, you know.

I will die if I stay much longer, and that will be useless to you. Let me go, and I will arrange for others to come back with me, others who know much more than I do. I am a simple pilot. I will bring you scientists.

We have no intention of hiding this knowledge from you, on the contrary, we have every reason to cooperate with you and do some joint projects. And we can supply the raw materials and the knowledge of how to turn it all to your advantage."

-"So since we are such good friends," said the second scientist, "tell me, where exactly is the home you speak of? Since you have lost the spaceship, obviously, we will have to take you there.'"

- "If I tell you, you will not understand and you will not be able to take me there, since it involves getting through additional dimensions.

Our scientists constructed our bases' entries like that, as a precaution against intruders. But if you take me back to Roswell, exactly where we crashed, I will find my own way."

"How will you do that?"

"Simple," said the Gray. "When a spacecraft lands on a particular spot, automatically it marks the spot, scans it, and sends data to our mission control for identification and location purposes. Thus, we are never lost. If I can contact my people, they will come for me."

"But if you go away, how do we communicate with you, and find out when the others are coming?"

"In the spacecraft there is a communication device. Let's go there. I am sure it is functional, because it is really indestructible. I'll teach you how to use it. We will contact my people from there and tell them about our plan. You will be there to supervise everything. Bring the boss, too, just in case."

The scientists looked at each other. They seemed rather pleased.

"Very well," said one of them. "We'll come back for you later tonight, after we talk to the boss. I am sure he will agree to our plan."
"It will be a feather in his cap," said the Gray, using an old fashioned human expression unexpectedly. The two scientists burst out laughing.

*** *** ***

And that, was indeed what happened. They took him back to Roswell, and left him there on the exact spot of the crash.
They did not leave the area, though, but hid in a small canteen which was placed at some distance, to watch what was going to happen to the Gray.
In a very short time, a spaceship came, landed, and he went in. The spaceship took off directly and vanished into the sky.
The scientists sent the piece of metal which the Gray had demonstrated with to a military laboratory, and they called one engineer from Lockheed Corporation and another one from MIT, to analyse the piece. Nobody could figure out what it was made of.
Still, prior to his departure, apparently the Gray did reveal many secrets of very advanced technology, that American corporations started developing right away, and began to use ten years later. Many highly advanced electronic gadgets that American consumers have used for a over a quarter of a century came from the Grays.

And what happened then?
A few years passed.
Then, a historic meeting happened. In February 1954, President Dwight Eisenhower went for a week's vacation to Palm Springs, California.
This was a little strange, and many did not quite understand the timing, because he just came back from a quail shooting vacation in Georgia. Actually, it was less than a week before his trip to Palm Springs.

On the night of February 20, 1954, the President of the United States disappeared

Two vacations in a row was not his style, but he went anyway, and arranged to stay there for a week.
Now, a president, as you know, is always surrounded by other officials, not to mention body guards; he is never out of sight.
But on the night of February 20, the President of the United States disappeared. The press, which somehow was alerted despite all the efforts for secrecy, spread rumors that he was ill, or that he had suddenly died.
The president's people were alarmed, so they called an emergency press conference, and announced that Eisenhower lost a tooth cap at his dinner, and had to be rushed to a dentist.
To make it more believable, the dentist was presented to the people.
He was invited to a function the next evening, and was introduced all around.
This, again, was strange.
Why would a dentist be invited to such an affair, and why would the President's personnel take such care to make him visible to everyone?

*** *** ***

A Cover-up!

It was a cover-up for the President's real business

Eisenhower was actually taken to Muroc Airfield, which was later renamed Edwards Air Force Base. There, he met with the Grays.
No president had ever done so before.
The delegation of the extraterrestrials consisted of eleven Grays. Six from Zeta Reticuli, and five from earth's underwater bases.
But of course, this was not their last meeting,

This marked only the beginning of negotiations between the government of United States and the Grays.
So the situation was no longer only in the hands of the military, but went much further.

*** *** ***

Eisenhower was the first American President to sign a treaty with the extraterrestrials.

Muroc Field/ Edwards Air Force Base.
Eisenhower was actually taken to Muroc Airfield, which was later renamed Edwards Air Force Base. There, he met with the Grays.

How was this meeting arranged, in the first place?

Before the meetings: Two major black projects

In 1953, astronomers discovered some large objects that at first were believed to be asteroids, and later proven to be spaceships. They were very large, but since they took a high orbit around the equator, they were not visible to laymen.
Two projects were installed:
- 1-**Project Sigma,** created to interpret the Grays' radio communications,
- 2-**Project Plato,** created to establish diplomatic relationships with the aliens.

There were talks about other races that contacted the humans at that time, arguments regarding who the treaties should be signed with, and so on.
As a matter of fact, the Nordics, a benevolent race, actually tried to prevent humans from getting into these evil treaties, and wanted them to dismantle their nuclear weapons and abandon their road to self destruction, but they were not listened to.
The Nordics wanted the humans to go on a path of spiritual development, but what the humans wanted was military secrets.
Because those humans were so badly contaminated, they would not even consider a peaceful offer.
And the treaty with the Grays was signed. It basically said that the aliens and the humans will not interfere in each other's affairs.

The humans will keep the alien presence a secret, and the Grays would be allowed to experiment on cows and on a limited number of human abductees. The abductees' names would be reported to the U.S. government for control, they were not to be harmed, and they should be returned to their homes after the memory of the events was removed.

But, as we know, the Grays did not keep their promise, and extended their experiments without telling the U.S. government.

They could not be trusted. But let's face it, the military people were treacherous as well. For example, there was the issue of the Gray who had arranged all of that.

Second meeting in 1954

He came back with a delegation in 1954, and agreed to stay on earth as a hostage of good will, on condition that he would be allowed the freedom to go back and forth to recharge himself.

This lasted for a year, but soon enough the military, having learned a little about the vicious plans of the Grays and the excessive number of abductions that was not agreed upon, turned back on their word to the hostage and locked him up for three years.

As a result, he developed extreme claustrophobia that eventually killed him, as they would not let him leave to recharge himself.

This information about Gray claustrophobia was never known about within the circle of ufologists.

*** *** ***

United States "Protocol on Extraterrestrials' Visit to Earth in 2022"

Master Kanazawa spoke about a very specific protocol written by the United States government. In the Kira'at provided below, you will have a short glance at its contents.

It might appear to many of you as a science fiction story, or a pure fabrication of mine, or a crazy scenario created by others who are deeply involved with this issue, but those who in the past were part of the team of American officials who met with extraterrestrials, and some of the military scientists who are currently working on joint extraterrestrials-intraterrestrials-Greys and American scientific and esoteric weapons systems programs, are fully aware of the existence of the secret governmental "Protocol on Extraterrestrials' Visit to Earth in 2022."

*** *** ***

It is up to you to take this subject into consideration, or disregard the whole idea.
But always ask yourself, what IF part of it is true? If I was not absolutely sure and certain that the "Protocol" indeed exists, and it is periodically and constantly reviewed and updated, I would have never dared to come forward and talk to you about it.
You do not have to be an insider to know about the "Protocol". Just ask any "avant-garde" futurist or an out-spoken quantum physics professor, if such a protocol could exist?
It is also my understanding that many Fire Chiefs in the United States, at one time in their career, have heard of, or were briefed on the instructions manual on how to deal with extraterrestrials should a landing (Assumed a hostile invasion) or encounter occur.

It is also my belief that the United States government published in March-April 1954, an instructions guide called "SOM1-01 Special Operations Manual: Extraterrestrial Entities and Technology, Recovery and Disposal." Some ufologists have claimed that "The cover of the manual includes the date April 1954 and notes that it was created by the "Majestic-12 Group." This is not correct. The manual was never written by that group.

What I do know is this, and this is the absolute truth: A group of scientists from MIT, Cal Tech, NSA, the United States Air Force, and top scientists from the United States Department of Energy (DOE) came up with the first draft of the manual.
A few years later, Reverend Billy Graham, and two powerful Catholic archbishops in the United States were called in to share their insights and express their concerns.
Part of what they had suggested appeared in the 15 page Addendum to "Protocol on Extraterrestrials' Visit to Earth in 2022."

Master Kanazawa in this part of his Kira'at did not address the issues of:
- **a**-The inevitable clash with extraterrestrials,
- **b**-The mass hysteria,
- **c**-The Aliens' Asphyxiation Effect (AAE), which is one of the United States government's major concerns,
- **d**-United States cities' evacuation,
- **e**-The manual of the United States government counter-attack measures against extraterrestrials' invasion.

But others, including Ambar Anati did!

Master Kanazawa's Kira'at (An excerpt):
- Following the initiative of the United States of America, a few countries are consulting with each other on the "Protocol on Extraterrestrials' Visit to Earth in 2022," written by the American government.

- The American Protocol is still in its infancy now. However, it is promising, because it is addressing subjects of extreme importance.
- It is both a protocol and an instructions manual.
- The Protocol part of it will remain in the hands of the governments, while the instructions manual will be made available to the people of Earth in 2021.
- However, leaks to the general public and the media beforehand are expected.

*** *** ***

Some of the issues discussed in the protocol and the manual are:

- 1-How an encounter with a pecies from outer space could affect the world economy, and Earth's monetary system. It is our belief that this issue is discussed in an addendum;
- 2-The question of God, and how to explain to human beings, the nature of God, and mainly the irrelevance and unnecessary existence of several organized religions, and religious governing bodies. It is our belief that this issue is discussed in an addendum;
- The Church of England, the Vatican, and a consortium of Christian Churches in the United States of America have joined in to draft the section related to the religious topics discussed in the American protocol;
- 3-The Ba'abs (Stargates), are a major issue, especially to the United States, Russia, China, France, Great Britain, and a few other countries that are going to emerge as a global power on the world market;
- However, the military aspects of the Ba'abs, mode of operation, and ramifications such as intergalactic travel, time-space travel, anti-matter, anti-gravity will be handled exclusively by the United States of America;

- 5-DNA contamination is another sensitive and extremely important issue.
  Human DNA contamination caused by excessive scientific and military genetic programs, that are not in the best interest of humanity.
  6-It is our belief that this very delicate subject has already been a part of previous meetings between American officials and an elite group of extraterrestrials;
- 7-The alien-human interbreeding programs: It is our belief that this very delicate subject has already been a part of previous meetings between American officials and an elite group of extraterrestrials;
- 8-The life and existence of the hybrid race on Earth.
- 9-It is our belief that this very delicate subject has already been a part of previous meetings between American officials and an elite group of extraterrestrials;
- 10-How to handle a close encounter with three different extraterrestrial races that are going to play a paramount role in the future of humanity;
- 11-Petrifying situations prompted by electric currents, and electricity stations and grid shortouts during the landing of the extraterrestrials ships on Earth;
- 12-The development of a global communications system, jointly administered by the Anunnaki, the United States of America, China, Russia, and Europe, for the purpose of informing the populations of Earth of the landing, the purpose of the landing, and areas of landings of the Anunnaki, and their Merkabah (Also Markaba) in several areas of the terrestrial globe.
- 13-This communications system will also be projected as a huge holographic screen that will appear in the sky, at close proximity to the surface of Earth, containing vital information intended to orient the people of the Earth.
- 14-You have to remember what we have said in the past, about the remaining portion of the people on Earth. Those who were saved, those who will perish, and those

who will not be allowed to ascend through the Ba'abs. The ascension through the Ba'abs is their only way of salvation.

United States Government Publications on Extraterrestrial Invasions

Do you think that alien invasion is a far fetched scenario?
Science fiction? Are you sure it will never happen? And hence forth, is 2022 and/ the return of the Anunnaki to earth a pure fantasy?
Well, think again, because the United States government is taking the issue of extraterrestrial threat and alien invasion very very seriously!! You bet!!
The United States government has published a series of books on the subject, and provided very detailed information and instruction on the danger of aliens, their threats, what to do if you encounter aliens, and what precaution and safety measures you should take.
Below, are some websites that have posted the government's publications, along with excerpts from each book.
We hope these websites will still be accessible to you, since "Big Brother" is constantly deleting/ adding sensitive material on the subject of UFOs and extraterrestrials.
We are referring to serious articles and summary findings by reliable authors, and not to the silly and ridiculous messages of fake mediums and spiritual extraterrestrial messengers-psychics on earth!!

1-Government Alien Invasion Plan:
You can read the instructions of the American government at:
www.scribd.com/doc/917802/Government-Publications-on-Aliens?query2=Government%20Alien%20Invasion%20Plan

2-Government Publications on Aliens and Security:
www.scribd.com/doc/917802/Government-Publications-on-Aliens?query2=government%20extraterrestrial

3-The United States Government's Plan with Aliens:
www.scribd.com/doc/917802/Government-Publications-on-Aliens?query2=the%20government's%20plan%20with%20aliens

4-United States National Defense Against Alien Invasions.
www.scribd.com/doc/917802/Government-Publications-on-Aliens?query2=national%20defense%20against%20aliens

5-Aliens' Attack Plan
scribd.com/doc/917802/Government-Publications-on-Aliens?query2=alien%20attack%20plan

6-What to Do in Case Of An Alien Attack
www.scribd.com/doc/917802/Government-Publications-on-Aliens?query2=what%20to%20do%20incase%20of%20alien%20attack

*** *** ***

PART TWO
The Return of the Anunnaki: Q&A

PART TWO
Q&A

Outlook for mankind after the year 2022
- Question: What is the outlook for mankind after the year 2022? You have explained this in some detail in your books but will we live in peace or does humankind still pose a threat to one another if challenges and greed are proposed like they always have been?
- Answer

Another extraterrestrial threat other than the Gray's aliens
- Question: After the Anunnaki's job is finished here on earth through decontamination will we ever have to deal with another extraterrestrial threat other than the Gray's aliens?
- Answer

On aliens competing with the Anunnaki to rule our planet
- Question: Are there any other alien races in this galaxy or another that could compete with the superstar status of the Anunnaki and rule our planet?
- Answer

Would the Anunnaki come to aid the planet if another alien threat happens?
- Question: You have said that the Anunnaki feel responsible for the hybrid contamination between the humans and the Gray's, would the Anunnaki ever come to the aid of the planet again if this threat would happen?
- Answer

- Question: Has the planet ever come close to another threat as serious as the Gray's and will it be a possibility?
- Answer

Hybrid Grays: Adoption and DNA contamination
- Question: Have there been a large number of ones that were disease free and human enough to be adopted?
- Answer
- Question: Could someone have a relative hybrid or be a child of a hybrid and not know it?
- Answer
- Question: I always wonder how people with no compassion what-so-ever are the same species. It seems that living as a loving and compassionate being is what our natural instinct wants us to do, so I wonder if hybrids have any connection to emotionless behavior?
- Answer
- Question: I have read the discussions about contaminated DNA and am curious to know if it is to the point where large amounts of people have some connection to hybrids?
- Answer
- Questions: Is it true that hybrid human/grey babies and children are being created and raised in secret bases?
- What of the stories of horrific experiments being performed on abducted humans in labs by the Greys as part of their breeding/tissue harvesting programs?
- Answer
- Question: What is the reason behind the Greys interbreeding program with humans?
- Answer
- Question: Is one of these Anunnaki Gods going to take over the earth after the pole shift?
- Answer

- Questions: I am very worried by what you have written on the subject of the return of the Anunnaki in 2022? Is it for real?
- Are they going to change the way we look?
- Are they going to get rid of us and replace us with a new human race
- What kind?
- Answer
- Question: Will the Anunnaki intervene to prevent possible use of atomic/thermonuclear weapons prior to, or during their return in 2022?
- Answer

Who will survive the return of the Anunnaki?
- Question: What percentage of the world's population will survive the return of the Anunnaki to become part of the new human race after 2022?
- Answer

How many other Anunnaki will be part of the return?
- Questions: Though the return will be led by Sinhars Marduchk and Inannaschamra, how many other Anunnaki will be part of the return?
- And how many Anunnaki guides will there be, for humans who will be saved and returned to earth after the cleansing?
- Answer

Efficient energy systems of the Anunnaki
- Question: What kind of clean and efficient energy systems, and modes of transportation will the Anunnaki introduce after 2022?
- Answer

Stargate over Chicago
- Question: Is there a stargate/ba'ab in Chicago?

- Where exactly is it located, and what does it look like? How would you jump into a ba'ab?
- Terminal of Grand Central Station in downtown Chicago
- Answer

Signs before the return of the Anunnaki
- Question: What are the signs that people will see in the skies the day before the Anunnaki return, and where will they be seen?
- Answer

Anunnaki's tools of annihilation
- Questions: Who/what created the "tool of annihilation" that the Anunnaki will use when they return?
- Answer

*** *** ***

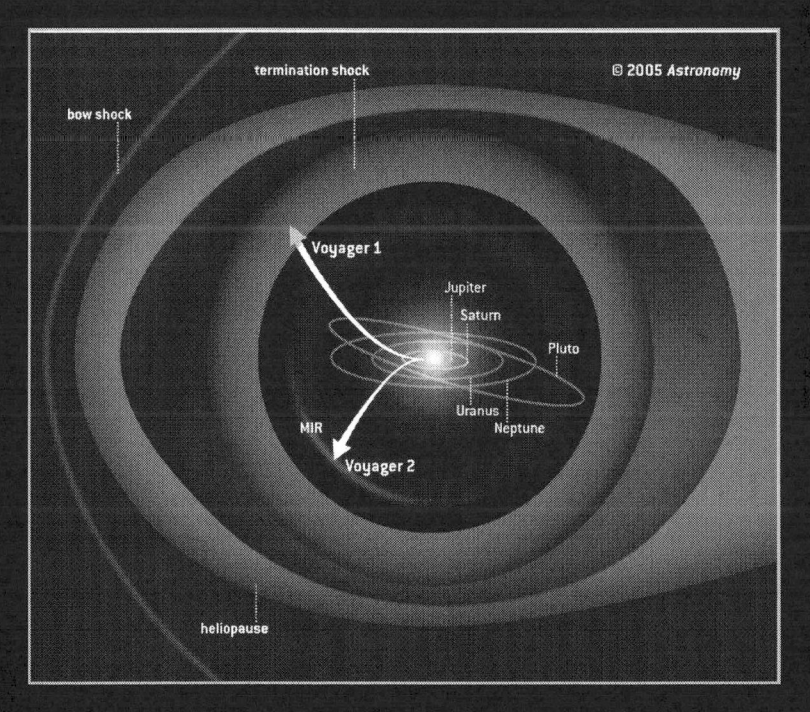

NASA's ring of hydrogen particles.

NASA has discovered a ring of hydrogen particles around our solar system–a protective layer, which is now being called the Heliosphere. This was announced by the Anunnaki-Ulema, centuries ago, and they called the ring "The Cosmic Plasmic Belt."

The Heliosphere is generated by solar wind particles, which originate deep within the Sun. NASA launched the Interstellar Boundary Explorer Mission (IBEX) last year to get a better picture of the Heliosphere.

It was always suspected that it existed, but NASA scientists thought it existed in a completely different form; instead of being a uniform stripe, there are bright spots, which indicate the "bubble" has varying intensity and density.

Also, though NASA knows it protects the solar system from the radiation outside of it, scientists still aren't entirely sure why it is there or what it does. As noted by NASA.

*** *** ***

2022 happenings are diverse, and could be easily misinterpreted by the public. Nothing physically will occur on Earth's landscape, or in its atmosphere.

A clash between a segment of non-terrestrials and humans is inevitable in the future.

In the past, more than 3 incidents occurred in secret military bases, and produced fatal consequences.

The incidents were provoked by military men who according to Greys' revelations have insulted Grey scientists who had worked on two joint- programs with the military.

The future clash will occur between the Anunnaki and the Greys, and humans will be caught in the middle. The outlook of mankind will be seriously affected by direct interference from the Anunnaki group called "Baalshamroot Ram".

This is the very group that surrounded the Solar System with the "Cosmic Plasmic Belt"; intense radiations/high velocity ranges of rays, as recently revealed by NASA.

The human race will never be in peace with itself, and with its own kind. This is dictated by the "Naf-Siya", the "Araya", the DNA and the bio-psychological makeup of human nature, originally created by the Anunnaki on two occasions:
The first time some 450,000 years ago, and the second time (Final Phase), some 10,000 years ago, which announced the dawn of civilizations on Earth.
Greed is an indivisible segment and one of the characteristics of the fabric of the human psyche. Thus, greed will always be here, and will increase the level of the contamination of mankind.
However, the year 2022 will bring major changes to social systems, and these changes will have enormous influence on the public's concept of religions.
Christianity's dogma could be altered. Islam will not be affected by these changes.
Buddhism, and Hinduism will not affected either, simply because Buddhism is founded on the concept of "Transmission of mind," and thus is not a religion per se.
Ancient Hinduism and Hindu manuscripts and inscriptions have already announced and pre-announced the existence of celestial spacecrafts known as "Vimanas" created by the "Gods", a super race from the multiple layers of the universe. Consequently, both will blend perfectly with the comprehension and definition of a new social order to be established by the Anunnaki.
In short, 2022 will bring paramount changes to:
a-Religions;
b-Social order.

*** *** ***

Another extraterrestrial threat other than the Gray's aliens

Question by Matt Hoxtell, Chicago, Illinois, USA.

Question: After the Anunnaki's job is finished here on earth through decontamination will we ever have to deal with another Extraterrestrial threat other than the Gray's aliens?

Answer:
The only threat humanity will face is the product of the Greys' agenda. It is important to understand, that the Greys have lived on Earth for millions of years, long before the human races were created by the Igigi, Anunnaki and Lyrans. We call the Greys "extraterrestrials".
This is not entirely correct, as the Greys are the intraterrestrials of Earth, and humans their co-habitants. We fear the Greys. And ironically, the Greys also fear us. They feel threatened by our nuclear arsenal and experiments, because these can annihilate Earth, where the Greys live. Earth is also the habitat of the Greys.
Earth is where their communities and families live.
Greys will do anything and everything to prevent humans from destroying Earth. Earth will be only destroyed by acts of nuclear war.
The Greys have adapted very well to the intra-landscape of Earth; meaning Inner-Earth. And water on Earth is essential for their survival and for "energizing" their crafts. Unfortunately, constant interactions with the Greys will deteriorate the genes of the human race.

The first phase of such deterioration is contamination.
The Anunnaki are fully aware of this contamination. Simply put, in order to eliminate the contamination of human and human DNA, the Anunnaki must get rid of the Greys. And the decontamination process will result in a major confrontation with the Greys. Some influential governments have already received a sort of "briefing" on the subject.

Some high officials took the threat very seriously, whilst many others did not. Their arrogance and ignorance will have lethal consequences, which humanity will suffer from.

No, there are no additional threats from other extraterrestrial races, simply because they are not interested in us. They are not interested, because we have nothing meaningful or important to offer them. Humans live on a linear scale. This is how and why we understand the universe in terms of time and distance/space. And this limits us, and prevents us from becoming members of the "Cosmic Federation."
Only two races in the known universe can live on Earth: The Anunnaki and the Greys. In the past three extraterrestrial races lived here on Earth, for sometime among us.
They were:
- **a**-The Anunnaki;
- **b**-The Lyrans;
- **c**-The Greys.

Their organisms and body structure could sustain our atmosphere and its conditions. Other extraterrestrials would not be able to live on Earth, as humans are not able to live on other known stars and planets because of their atmospheric conditions. Other alien races will self-destruct if they try to live on Earth.
Consequently, they have no interest whatsoever in invading or dominating Earth. In other words, the only threat, the only real threat, will come from the Greys.
But for the time being, we are safe, because the Greys still need us. Despite their highly advanced technology and science, the Greys did not yet find the perfect and final formula for saving themselves, genetically.

For some incomprehensible and possibly silly reasons, the survival of the Greys depends on two things:
- **a**-The survival of humans;
- **b**-The safety of planet Earth.

*** *** ***

Aliens competing with the Anunnaki to rule our planet?

Question by Matt Hoxtell, Chicago, Illinois, USA.

Question: Are there any other alien races in this galaxy or another that could compete with the superstar status of the Anunnaki and rule our planet?
Answer:
On the market nowadays, we find several encyclopedias and field-guides on extraterrestrial races.
The Internet is infested with silly and childish websites posting ridiculous literature on extraterrestrial races, description of their physiognomy, heights, weights, eyes, skin, etc. This is nonsense par excellence. How did they know about these extraterrestrial races?

What are their sources, data, and authoritative references?
They are non-existent. Their articles are the product of an erroneous imagination and immature fantasy.
Unless you break the frontiers of time and space, and land on their planets and stars, you will never be able to learn about their species, physiognomy and their biological structure on any level.
As long as modern ufology embraces such phantasmagoric assumptions and fake narratives, ufology will never be accepted academically, or gain the respect and trust of erudite milieus and scientists.
However, and according to some statements and "leaks", we have learned about the existence of six different extraterrestrial races who have contacted the United States military.
This was mentioned in the "Krill File".
But again, this so-called file was announced to the ufology community by Mr. Moore, who has been discredited by eminent ufologists.
And once again, I ask you to define what we understand by "Eminent ufologists"?
How eminence is defined, and on what basis or foundation, such eminence is based upon and structured?

To tell you the truth, nobody knows, except the Anunnaki-Ulema. Unless you are familiar with Ana'kh, and have read the archaic manuscripts of the Anunnaki-Ulema, and some of the Phoenician cosmogeny tablets, and unless you are familiar with the Akkadian and proto-Mesopotamian language(s), you will never be able –for sure– to categorize the galactic races.

All we have is mythology and colorful folklore. And beginning in the early 1950's, authors began to put their spin on everything extraterrestrial or alien. Call it science fiction, or perhaps mytho-inspirational essay, but not an authoritative study of galactic civilizations.

As of today, we are aware of the existence of two races:

a-The Greys;

b-The Anunnaki.

The Greys became known to us through articles by all sorts of ufologists, contactees (usually phony/fake), abductees, charlatan channelers, statements by so-called military men who worked in secret military bases, "insiders" and self-serving authors.

The truth I tell you, is that the Greys do exist, but they are not, who, what and how they are generally described to be, by many ufologists and those who claim to have had any sort of contact or rapport with them.

In some cases, accounts of encounters were correct, but in general, 95% of accounts and reports betray the truth, simply because the human mind is unable to understand what flashes before our eyes.

And this apparent in the way contactees/abductees (followed by a fleet of ufologists) describe the Greys. For instance, how many times have you heard from abductees and ufologists alike, that the Greys or extraterrestrials have very big eyes in proportion to the size of their heads, and the eyes were described as large eyes slanted upward and outward, or big dark eyes that were olive or almond-shaped?

Many times, I'm sure.

To tell you the truth, extraterrestrials' eyes are as big or as small as human eyes. And their sockets are almost similar to ours, but with three major differences. One of them is the retina. Aliens do not have retina in their eyes, simply because they do not need one.

Abductees were not able to realize that aliens or extraterrestrials eyes were "masked."

By masked I mean their eyes were covered by a dark lens or more exactly a screen, called "Bou-Ka'h" in the Ana'kh, the Anunnaki language. The large black eyes were simply a dark screen applied to the eyes of the extraterrestrials.

Consider this screen as eyeglasses for now (But in actuality these glasses provided the alien with information, much like glasses with mini TV/info screens on them being made and used by the military today). This common error is clearly shared by ufology authors, ufologists, and researchers alike.

This serious misconception and erroneous description are strong evidence that we have no clear vision or understanding of the physiognomy of extraterrestrials.

If this is true, then we are not in a position to categorize and adequately classify aliens, extraterrestrials, and Greys.

Thus, recognizing and/or defining other extraterrestrial species is pure speculation.

In conclusion, we should concentrate exclusively on two known non-human races; the Anunnaki and the Greys.

Such concentration will enable us to conclude that:
- 1-There are no other extraterrestrials on the scene;
- 2-The Greys are not in any position to compete with the Anunnaki.

And since we have logically eliminated the possible interference from other alien races (non-humans) that exist in our galaxy/other galaxies answering the question: "Are there any other alien races in this galaxy or another that could compete with the superstar status of the Anunnaki and rule our planet?" becomes an easy task.

And the answer is: The Greys cannot rule our planet, nor can they challenge the super status of the Anunnaki for obvious reasons.

One of these reasons is the fact that the Anunnaki are far more advanced than the Greys.

*** *** ***

Would the Anunnaki come to aid the planet if another threat happens?

Questions by Matt Hoxtell, Chicago, Illinois, USA.

Question: You have stated that the Anunnaki feel responsible for hybrid contamination between humans and the Gray's, would the Anunnaki ever come to the aid of the planet aif this threat would happen again?
Answer:
Yes and yes.
This was basically the topic Sinhar Ambar Anati (Victoria) discussed with representatives from the United States government years ago. Please refer to the book: "Anunnaki Ultimatum", co-authored by Ilil Arbel. Anati made it clear to American scientists and to two generals, that the Greys' contamination will inevitably destroy the human race.

*** *** ***

Question: Has the planet ever come close to another threat as serious as the Gray's and will it be a possibility?
Answer:
Yes, millions of years ago, when a huge celestial object was on a trajectory in the direction of planet Earth.
The Anunnaki deviated the object from its collision course with Earth. And later on, they decided to surround the Solar system with a protection shield, known as "The Cosmic Plasmic Belt", which is called "Zinar" in Ana'kh, the Anunnaki language. This was also mentioned in the Book of Ramadosh "Ketab Rama-Dosh."

*** *** ***

Hybrid Grays:
Adoption and DNA contamination

Questions from Melanie Schmidt:

Question: Have there been a large number of hybrids that were disease free and human enough to be adopted?
Answer:
Yes. A few hybrids were adopted, usually by military families, and the adoptive parents must go to the base where the hybrids are, and can select the one they will adopt. This is a fact.

Basically, some infant-hybrids look just like our own children.
No physical deformities whatsoever.
However, they have shown some muscular anomalies right below their shoulder plates and the vertebral column in the neck. They cannot turn their heads effortlessly.

Another thing: They will never grow to be tall.
Their average height is 5ft 6"

Question: Could someone have a hybrid relative or be the child of a hybrid and not know it?
Answer:
No. Impossible.

Question: I always wonder how people with no compassion whatsoever are the same species.
It seems that living as a loving and compassionate being is what our natural instinct wants us to do, so I wonder if hybrids have any connection to emotionless behavior?
Answer:
Many infant hybrids have displayed high degree of emotion, attachment, fear, joy and anxiety, and become very attached to their parents.

Question: I've read discussions about contaminated DNA and am curious if it is to the point where large numbers of people have some connection to hybrids?
Thanks! Melanie Schmidt.

Answer:
No, not many. Those are very rare cases.
Worth mentioning here is that not all infant hybrids have contaminated DNA.
The contamination occurs during the interbreeding process. If noticed by the Grays, they will dispose of those children right away. This has been documented and reported by abductees who lived for a while in the hybrids' habitat.
Dr. David Jacobs wrote a magnificent book on the subject called "Threat". I encourage you to read his book, as it is really fascinating. In fact, a few years ago I contacted Dr. Jacobs, and asked his permission to use some of his material. And gracefully he agreed.

*** *** ***

Questions from Elaine Bradley, New York, New York:

Question: Is it true that hybrid human/grey babies and children are being created and raised in secret bases?
What of the stories of horrific experiments being performed on abducted humans in labs by the Greys as part of their breeding/tissue harvesting programs?

Answer:
Once again Maximillien de Lafayette has provided us with an account of the unthinkable horrors committed by the Greys, as witnessed by Sinhar Anbar Anati:
Here is her account (in her own words), on visiting the Hybrids:

My first encounter with the hybrid children, and my first glimmer of understanding of what eternity is like.

133

"The base we are visiting today is under water," said Sinhar Inannaschamra. "We are about to descend way down into the Pacific."

"What about air?" I asked, a bit apprehensive about the idea. Surely Sinhar Inannaschamra won't forget I could not breathe under water, but still…

"We pass through a lock that is safe for both water and air," said Sinhar Inannaschamra, "and inside, it's geared for the hybrids, which, just like humans, need air." In a few minutes, we stopped and I assumed, correctly, that we were already inside the base.

"They are expecting us," said Sinhar Inannaschamra. "Don't worry about them. They know I can blow the whole place up if they dare to give me any trouble."

The spaceship's door opened and I saw that we were inside a huge, hangar-like room. If I had expected a beautiful, aquarium-like window, showing the denizens of the deep playing in their blue environment, I would have been disappointed. But knowing the Grays, I expected nothing of the sort, and so the beige and gray room, all metal and lacking any windows, did not exactly surprise me.

"This base is enormous, you know" said Sinhar Inannaschamra. "It is used for many operations, but we will just concentrate on the hybrids today."

I was pleased to hear that, since I was secretly apprehensive about the possibility of stumbling on one of the Grays' hellish laboratories. I will never forget, or forgive, what I saw in their lab. But I said nothing and waited to see what was going to happen next. Sinhar Inannaschamra walked me to a solid wall, put her hand on it, and the wall shimmered a little, then moved, allowing a door to form and open for us.

We entered a long corridor, illuminated by stark, white light, with many regular doors on each side.

Sinhar Inannaschamra opened one of the doors and we entered a large room, obviously a refectory since it contained extremely long tables, all made of metal. The room was painted entirely in beige – tables, chairs, walls, and ceiling, and had no windows. It was scrupulously clean.

Suddenly, the tables opened up, each table revealing a deep groove on each of its long sides. Plates of what seemed to be normal human food were released from the grooves, and placed before each chair. At this moment, a few doors opened at various parts of the room, and from each door an orderly file of children came in and settled at the table.

They were completely silent, not a word was heard, as they picked up their forks and began to eat. None of them paid any attention to us, even though we stood there in plain view of them.

The children seemed to range from six to twelve, but it was difficult to be sure of that. On the one hand, they were small and fragile, so I might have mistaken their ages. On the other, their eyes gave the impression almost of old age.

They seemed wise beyond their tender years. Their hair was thin, their skin was pale to gray, and they all wore white clothes of extreme cleanliness.

Despite these similarities, which made them look as if they were all related to each other, I could tell some differences between them that seemed rather fundamental. It was almost as if they fitted within three distinct groups. I mentioned it, in a whisper, to Sinhar Inannaschamra, and she nodded.

"Yes, you got it," she said. "They consist of early-stage hybrids, middle-stage hybrids, and late-stage hybrids. The first group is born from the first combination of abductees' and Grays' DNA. They closely resemble the Grays.

Look at their skin – the grayish color is very close to that of the Grays, and so is the facial structure. The second group, the middle-stage hybrids, are the result of mating between these early-stage ones, once they are old enough for reproduction, and human abductees.

The resulting DNA is closer to humans, and so they look much more like humans, and many of them lose the Progeria gene.

The third group, the late-stage hybrid, is the most important. Middle-stage hybrids are mated with humans to create them – and they can hardly be distinguished from humans."

"Yes, I can tell who the late-stagers are quite easily," I said. "But there are not too many of them here, right?"

"This is true, not too many are here. A large number of these hybrids, who represent the most successful results of the experiments, are placed for adoption with human families."

"Are the human families aware of the origin of their children?"

"Yes, in most cases they are. Generally, they are adopted by a high-ranking United States military man or woman, who had worked, or still works, with aliens, in secret military bases. This happens much more often than most people suspect… the spouse of the military person may or may not know, depending on the circumstances and character traits of the hybrid child. These lucky hybrids lead a much better life than whose who are raised in places like this one, communally."

"Are they badly treated here? Are they abused by the Grays?"

"No, the Grays don't want to lose them, they are too valuable. But they receive no love, no individual attention, there is no real parenting, and the environment is barren and depressing. They live like that until they are old enough to be of use in the experiments. Not a very nice life for any child."

"And what about the issue of Progeria? I mean, for the adopted ones?"

"Only the hybrids who are entirely free of Progeria are adopted by human families. We even suspect, though we are not sure, that many of the Progeria stricken late-stagers are killed, since their Progeria gene is too strong. The Grays believe that after these three attempts, it cannot be eradicated by further breeding."

"And so they kill the poor things… what is the motive for all these atrocities?"

"All for the same reason I have mentioned before. They think they somehow will save their civilization. But they are doomed."

"But in the meantime, they harm, torture, and kill so many people. I don't understand why it is tolerated." Sinhar Inannaschamra did not answer.

*** *** ***

The children finished eating, still in complete silence. Each child, as he or she finished his/her meal, leaned back into the chair, and as soon as all of them were leaning back, the groove from which the plates came opened up, and re-absorbed all the plates. "They now go to an automatic dishwashing machine," explained Sinhar Inannaschamra.

The children got up, and left the dismal room in the same file arrangement they came in. As soon as the room was empty, large vacuum cleaners emerged from the wall and sucked up every crumb, every piece of debris. Then they sprayed the tables and floor with a liquid that smelled like disinfectant. The room was spotlessly clean again, ready for the next sad, depressing meal.

"Shall we go to the dormitories now?" asked Sinhar Inannaschamra. I nodded. We followed the children through one of the doors, and entered a place that was a combination of an old-fashioned orphanage and military barracks.

It was a very large room, but the ceiling was not high, only about twelve feet. Again, everything was beige and gray, and there were no windows to relieve the monotony.

The room was full of beds, arranged above each other in groups of three, like in a submarine. Dozens and dozens of such rows seemed to stretch to a very long distance.

The beds were made of some metal, very smooth, and of silver-gray color. They seemed to be assembled like prefab furniture.

"Sinhar Inannaschamra," I said, "there are no ladders. How do the children reach the upper levels?"

"They can levitate," said Sinhar Inannaschamra. "Look at this. Part of each bed is magnetic, so each child can have his or her toys attached to it. As for the lower beds, the toys are stored next to them."

"So they have toys," I said. "That's a mercy."

"Yes, the Grays discovered that mental stimulation is highly important to the hybrids' development. There are plenty of other activities, mostly with abductees, that relieve their lives of the tedium, at least to a certain extent."

"But they have no privacy at all."

"None whatsoever, they only get their own room when they are more mature, but they have one thing that pleases them. If the children want to, they can put their things in their bed, close the bed with a panel, and hide it inside a wall. They like that."

"I wonder, too, is it a comfort for them to be together, after all?"

"Their feelings and emotional state are not exactly human… it's hard to explain. I think it's time for you to see them interact."

"Where are all the children now?"

"They are attending various activities," said Sinhar Inannaschamra. "Come, I'll show you."

We entered a room that opened directly from the dormitory. To my surprise, it was really a glass bubble. You could see the outside, which was an unpleasant desert surrounding. I found it nasty, but I figured that to the children it might represent a pleasant change.

About ten children, seemingly between the ages of six and eight, sat on the ground, which was simply desert sand. They were playing with normal human toys – trucks, cars, and trains. They filled the things with sand, using plastic trowels that one usually sees on the beach.

They were also building tunnels from the sand, wetting it with water from large containers that stood here and there. They seemed to be enjoying their games, certainly concentrating on them, but their demeanor remained quiet and subdued, and they did not engage in the laughter, screaming, yelling, or fighting that children of this age normally do.

"They also have rooms with climbing equipment, and places to play ball," said Sinhar Inannaschamra. "It is needed to strengthen their bones and muscles."

I approached the children, a little apprehensively, worried that I might frighten the poor things. They looked up at me, seemingly waiting for me to do something, but I was pleased to realize that they were not afraid. I sat on the sand, took some stones that were scattered around, and arranged them so that they created a little road.

The children stared at me for a minute with their strange, wise eyes, as if trying to read my thoughts, and almost instantly grasped the idea and continued to build the road together.

None of them smiled, but they seemed very much engaged in the new activity. Once all the stones were used, they looked at me again, as if trying to absorb information, and sure enough, after a minute they took the trucks and made them travel down the little road. I got up and let them play.

"So they can read minds," I said to Inannaschamra.

"To an extent," she said. "At this age, they basically just absorb images you project. You probably thought about the trucks going on this road, and they saw it."

"And everything was done together, as if they were mentally connected," I said. "Do they do everything together?"

"Yes, everything is communal, even the bathrooms where they clean themselves. But don't be too upset about it. If they are separated from each other before adolescence, they become extremely upset. It is almost as if the onset of puberty makes them an individual, and before that they have a group mentality."

"Horrible," I said.

"They are not unhappy," said Sinhar Inannaschamra. "Only as adolescents, when they break off the communal mind, do they come to understand how unhappy they really are. But we will visit the adolescents on another occasion."

"Very well," I said.

"Would you like to see the room where they keep the fetuses?" asked Sinhar Inannaschamra.

I followed Sinhar Inannaschamra to the corridor, and we walked quite a distance before opening another door. We entered another one of the hangar-sized rooms, full of tanks.

"Each tank contains liquid nutrients," said Sinhar Inannaschamra. "This is where they put the fetuses, as soon as they are removed from the abductees. The tanks are arranged in order, from the youngest fetuse,s to those that are almost ready to be removed."

"Do they separate them into stages?" I asked.

"Yes, this room is for early stagers only. In other rooms, they have the middle stagers. But the late stagers remain in the mother's womb until birth, to make them as close to humans as possible."

"And what are the babies like?"

"Quiet, not as responsive as human babies.

Many of them die as soon as they are removed from the tank. Those that survive are generally mentally well developed, but physically weak, and emotionally subdued."

"And who takes care of them?"

"Both Grays and abductees. The Grays perform most of the physical requirements, but the abductees supply the human touch. We can't go there yet."

"How come?"

"We need to prepare you to interact with abductees. They are very complicated. We shall have a few sessions about interacting with them at the same time when we teach you how to work with the adolescents.

Also, you had wanted some instruction on how to contact and help those people that are children of humans and Anunnakis, like your son. This requires some teaching, too."

We went back to our spaceship, not saying much. I remember thinking that if I were part of the Anunnaki Council, I would vote to kill every Gray in the known universe. Of course I did not say it to Sinhar Inannaschamra, but I am sure she knew how I felt. Back home, I went to my beloved garden and sat under a tree that constantly showered tiny blossoms on me, like little snowflakes. I did not even know I was crying.

"What is the matter?" said Marduchk, who suddenly appeared next to me. I told him about the visit with the hybrids.

"The hybrids are not abused," said Marduchk. "Something else is bothering you."

I thought for a moment, and then decided I might as well be honest with him. "Yes," I said. "I cannot understand the Anunnaki's casual attitude about the fact that thousands of human beings are tortured and killed all the time.

Neither you nor Sinhar Inannaschamra seem to be as shocked as I am about the fact that the Grays engage in such atrocities."

Marduchk was quiet for a minute, thinking. At this conversation, we did not use the Conduit, because in my agitated state I found it difficult. I was not entirely used to it as yet. So I waited for him to say what he thought.

"I see your point," he said. "You think we are callous about it."

"Yes, I do, to tell you the truth. Why don't you destroy the Grays? Why do you allow so much death, so much pain? Are you, after all, cruel beings? Have you become callous because you have lived so many years, and become thick-skinned about suffering?"

"No, we are not cruel. It's just that we view life and death differently than you do. We cannot destroy all the Grays, even if we wanted to. We don't commit genocide, even if they try to do it. We don't want to kill them. We know that they will die on their own."

"And in the meantime, suffering means nothing to you?"

"It means a lot, but destroying the Grays would not eliminate suffering that occurs in all the universes we go to. There are other species that are even worse than the Grays, you just don't know about them because their horrific behavior is not aimed at humans."

"It seems to me, that even though you are so much more sophisticated than humans, the fact that you deny the existence of God may have deprived you of your ethics, after all."

"Deny God? What makes you think we deny God?" asked Marduchk. He seemed genuinely surprised.

"Marduchk, you have told me, more than once, that the Anunnaki created the human race, not God. So where is God if He is not the Creator? Your statements are contradictory."

"Not at all," said Marduchk. "The Anunnaki view of God is similar to human religions in many ways, but contains much more information.

The term we use to describe God is 'All That Is.' To the Anunnaki, God is made of inexhaustible mental energy, and contains all creation within Itself, therefore representing a gestalt of everything that has existed, exists now, or will exist in the future, and that includes all beings, all known universes, and all events and phenomena.

God's dearest wish is to share in the lives of all its creations, learn and experience with them, and from them. But while they are imperfect, God Itself is perfect, which is why It can only be seen as a gestalt."

"Why are you calling God *It*?" I asked.

"Because we do not attribute gender to God."

"I see," I said. "So in essence, the Anunnaki God is not all that different from ours. What else should I know?"

"It is possible that other primary energy gestalts existed before God came into being, and actually created It. If so, then the possibility exists that there are many Gods, all engaged in magnificent creativity within their own domains.

We are not certain if that is so, but we do not dismiss this beautiful possibility."

"That is vastly different from human thought," I said, meditating. "But how does it tie in with life and death issues, and with the fact that you have created us?"

"The individuals that exist within God, though part of God, have free will and self-determination. In life and in death, each is a part of God and also a complete and separate individual that will never lose its identity.

The Anunnaki are indeed the creators of human beings, but since each Anunnaki is a part of God, there is no conflict in the idea of their creation of humanity.

Creation is endless and on-going, and human beings, in their turn, create as well – for example, great art, literature, and service to other people, animals, and the planet Earth – though they do not exactly create life as yet. We are all part of the grand gestalt, and that makes All That Is such an apt name for God."

"So how does that make the situation with the Grays' atrocities any better?"

"It is better because the lives that they take are not disappearing into a void. Each individual is eternal, and even if killed as a child, will go on into other domains. I am not saying that this justifies the Grays' atrocities.

I am merely pointing out that even though these atrocities do exist, the individuals affected will have another chance."

"Yes, this does make a difference, and I can see how it would affect your thinking. But for me, after seeing what the Grays do to humans in their labs, it is still very disturbing."

"I can understand that, Victoria. It is not something you are accustomed to. Tell me, do you still want to do this mission?" He asked his question in a very neutral way, obviously not wanting to influence my free will.

"Yes, more than ever," I said. "Maybe I can do some good for these poor, sad children."

"I have a suggestion, then," said Marduchk. "I don't see it as a long-term mission, since you cannot change the ways of the Grays from within. I think you will find it a springboard to other missions, as it is obvious to me that you have some thoughts on making the Anunnaki do something about the Grays to force them to stop their experiments.

Doing this mission will be extremely good as a learning experience, right from inside the Grays' base. As for contacting the people who are the children of humans and Anunnaki's, that will not take much of your time.

There are very few of these around, these days."

"How long do you think this mission will take me?"

"Exactly nine months," said Marduchk. I stared for a minute and then laughed.

"I see what you mean, Marduchk. You think I should start our daughter, allow her to grow in the tube in the Anunnaki fashion, and while she is in the tube, concentrate on my mission. Then, I should come back and spend some time with you and the baby, before embarking on other missions."

"Doesn't it sound like a good plan? While the baby is in the tube, there is nothing you can do for her other than look at her as she grows. And you can easily do that with a monitor from earth, right from the Grays' base. And we will talk every day, so if you have any concerns about her, I can take care of it."

"This is a wonderful idea," I said. "I will have the orientation regarding the abductees and the adolescent hybrids, and of course the human-Anunnaki people, and when I am ready to go on my mission, I will first stop at the hospital and start the baby!"

This plan made me feel a little better, but I knew I must give the issue some more thought, and perhaps further discussion. So, when I went to see Sinhar Inannaschamra the next day to arrange for the orientation, I brought the subject up with her, and told her honestly how I felt.

"Yes, I do understand how you feel, Victoria," she said. "Before we do any more work with the hybrid mission, I would like to give you a little background about our relationship to life and death."

"I would very much welcome it," I said.

"So let's start with the concept of An-Hayya'h," said Sinhar Inannaschamra.

"I have never heard the word mentioned," I said.

"This word, which is also used as A-haya and Aelef-hayat, could be the most important word in Anakh, our language, as well as in the written history of humanity, because it deals with several extremely important issues.

These are:
- The origin of humans on earth.
- How humans are connected to the Anunnaki.
- Importance of water to humans and Anunnaki.
- The life of humans.
- Proof that it was originally a woman who created man, Adam and the human race, via her Anunnaki identity.
- The return of the Anunnaki to earth.
- Humanity's hopes and salvation, and a better future for all, our gifts to you, as your ancestors and creators."

"Complicated concepts," I said.

"I will try to explain the whole concept as clearly as possible, because it is extremely difficult to find the proper and accurate word or words in terrestrial languages and vocabularies. Let's start with the word itself. The word An-Hayya'h is composed of two parts. The first part is 'An' or 'A' (Pronounced Aa), or 'Aelef' (pronounced a'leff).

It is the same letter in Anakh, Akkadian, Canaanite, Babylonian, Assyrian, Ugaritic, Phoenician, Moabite, Siloam, Samaritan, Lachish, Hebrew, Aramaic, Nabataean Aramaic, Syriac, and Arabic.

All these languages are derived from Ana'kh. Incidentally, the early Greeks adopted the Phoenician Alphabet, and Latin and Cyrillic came from the Greek Alphabet. The Hebrew, Aramaic and Greek scripts all came from the Phoenician. Arabic and most of the Indian scriptures came from the Aramaic.

The entire Western World received its language from the Phoenicians, the descendants of the Anunnaki. Anyway, the 'An in Ana'kh means one of the following:

- Beginning
- The very first
- The ultimate
- The origin
- Water

On earth, this word became Alef in Phoenician, Aramaic, Hebrew, Syriac and Arabic. Alef is the beginning of the alphabet in these languages. In Latin, it's 'A' and in Greek it is Alpha. In Hebrew, the Aleph consists of two yuds (pronounced Yod); one yod is situated to the upper right and the other yod to the lower left. Both yods are joined by a diagonal vav.

They represent the higher water and the lower water, and between them the heaven.

This mystic-kabalistic interpretation was explained before by Rabbi Isaac Luria. Water is extremely important in all the sacred scriptures, as well as in the vast literature and manuscripts of extraterrestrials and the Anunnaki.

Water links humans to the Anunnaki. In the Babylonian account of Creation, Tablet 1 illustrates Apsu (male), representing the primeval fresh water, and Tiamat (female), the primeval salt water.

These two were the parents of the gods. Apsu and Tiamat begat the Lahmu (Lakhmu) and Lahamu (Lakhamu) deities.

In the Torah, the word 'water' was mentioned on the first day of the creation of the world: 'And the spirit of God hovered over the surface of the water.' In the Chassidut, the higher water is 'wet' and 'warm,' and represents the closeness to Yahweh (God), and it brings happiness to man.

The lower water is 'cold,' and brings unhappiness because it separates us from Yahweh, and man feels lonely and abandoned. The Ten Commandments commence with the letter

Alef: 'Anochi (I) am God your God who has taken you out of the land of Egypt, out of the house of bondage.'

The letter 'Alef' holds the secret of man, his/her creation, and the whole universe, as is explained in the Midrash. In Hebrew, the numeric value of Aleph is 1.

And the meaning is:
- First
- Adonai
- Leader
- Strength
- Ox
- Bull
- Thousand
- Teach.

According to Jewish teachings, each Hebrew letter is a spiritual force and power by itself, and comes directly from Yahweh. This force contains the raw material for the creation of the world and man.

The Word of God ranges from the Aleph to the Tav, which is the last letter in the Hebrew alphabet. In Revelation 1:8, Jesus said: 'I am Alpha and Omega, the beginning and the ending.' In John 1:1-3, as the Word becomes Jesus, the Lord Jesus is also the Aleph and the Tav, as well as the Alpha and the Omega.

In Him exists all the forces and spiritual powers of the creation. Jesus is also connected to water, an essential substance for the purification of the body and the soul, which is why Christians developed baptism in water.

In Islam, water is primordial and considered the major force of the creation of the universe. The Prophet Mohammad said, as can be read in the Quran: 'Wa Khalaknah Lakoum min al Ma'i, koula chay en hay,' meaning: 'And We (Allah) have created for you from water everything alive.'

The Islamic numeric value of Aleph and God is 1. To the Anunnaki and many extraterrestrial civilizations, the An or Alef represents the number 1, also Nibiru, the constellation Orion, the star Aldebaran, and above all the female aspect of creation symbolized in an Anunnaki woman 'Gb'r, whom you know as the Angel Gabriel on earth."

"The Angel Gabriel was a woman?" I asked, amazed.

"Unquestionably so," said Sinhar Inannaschamra, smiling.

"How interesting," I said. "But do go on. What about the second part of the word An-Hayya'h?"

"The second part, namely the Hayya'h part, means:
- Life
- Creation
- Humans
- Earth, where the first human, which was a female, was created.
-

In Arabic, Hebrew, Aramaic, Turkish, Syriac, and so many Eastern languages, the Anunnaki words Hayya'h and Hayat mean the same thing: Life. But the most striking part of our story is that the original name of Eve, the first woman, is not Eve, but Hawwa, derived directly from Hayya. You see, Eve's name in the Bible is Hawwa, or Chavvah.

In the Quran it is also Hawwa, and in every single Semitic and Akkadian script, Eve is called Hawwa or Hayat, meaning the giver of life, the source of the creation.

Now, if we combine An with Hayya'h or Hayat, we get these results: Beginning; The very first; The ultimate; The origin; Water + Life; Creation; Humans; Earth, where the first was created; Woman. And the whole meaning becomes: The origin of the creation, and first thing or person who created the life of humans was a woman, or water. Amazingly enough, in Anakh, woman and water mean the same thing.

Woman represents water according to the Babylonian, Sumerian and Anunnaki tablets, as clearly written in the Babylonian-Sumerian account of Creation, Tablet 1."

"Well, no wonder then, that God has no gender in the Anunnaki concept," I said. "I found that very interesting, when Marduchk told me about All That Is as the name of God."

"Yes, it all ties together rather nicely, even if it is a little complicated," said Sinhar Inannaschamra.

"A little?" I said, laughing. "I will have to think about this for a long time before I am comfortable with the concepts. But it is fascinating. I would like, moreover, to understand a little better how the Anunnaki created the human race."

"Well, it happenned around 65,000 B.C.E," said Sinhar Inannaschamra. The Anunnaki, at that time, lived in the regions you now call Iraq, known then as Mesopotamia, Sumer and Babylon, and also Lebanon, known as Loubnan, Phoenicia, or Phinikia. We taught your ancestors how to write, speak, play music, build temples, and navigate, as well as geometry, algebra, metallurgy, irrigation, and astronomy, among other arts.

We had high hopes for this race, which we have created in our image. But the human race disappointed us almost from the beginning, for human beings were, and still are, cruel, violent, greedy and ungrateful.

So, we gave up on you and left earth.

The few remaining Anunnaki living in Iraq and Lebanon were killed by savage military legions from Greece, Turkey and other nations of the region.

The Anunnaki left earth for good, or at least that was the plan at the time. Other extraterrestrial races came to earth, but these celestial visitors were not friendly and considerate like the Anunnaki.

The new extraterrestrials had a different plan for humanity, and their agenda included abduction of women and children, animal mutilation, genetic experiments on human beings, creating a new hybrid race, etc..."

"But you are still there, Sinhar Inannaschamra. And you are still trying to help. Obviously, you would not have projects such as you had with me if you had forgotten us…"

"No, we did not totally forget you. We could not... After all, many of your women were married to Anunnaki, and some of our women were married to humans.

Ancient history, the Bible, Sumerian Texts, Babylonian scriptures, Phoenician tablets, and historical accounts from around the globe did record these events. You can find them, almost intact, in archeological sites in Iraq and Lebanon, as well as in museums, particularly the British Museum, the Iraqi Museum and the Lebanese Museum."

"So how did you keep in touch with human civilization?"

"Before leaving you, we activated in your cells the infinitesimally invisible multi-multi-microscopic gene of An-Hayya'h.

Yes, this is how it is all inter-connected... It was implanted in your organism and it became a vital component of your DNA. Humans are not yet aware of this, just as they were unaware of the existence of their DNA for thousands of years. As your medicine, science and technology advance, you will be able, some day, to discover that miniscule, invisible, undetectable An-Hayya'h molecule, exactly as you have discovered your DNA.

An-Hayya'h cannot be detected yet in your laboratories. It is way beyond your reach and your comprehension, but it is extremely powerful, because it is the very source of your existence. Through An-Hayya'h, we remained in touch with you, even though you are not aware of it.

It is linked directly to a 'Conduit' and to a 'Miraya' (monitor/mirror) on Ashtari (Nibiru). Every single human being on the face of the earth is linked to the outer-world of the Anunnaki through An-Hayya'h. And it is faster than the speed of light.

It reaches the Anunnaki through 'Ba'abs' (star gates). It travels the universe and reaches the 'Miraya' of the Anunnaki through the Conduit, which was integrated in your genes and your cerebral cells by the Anunnaki some 65,000 years ago."

"The same Conduit I have now?"

"Yes, that same Conduit. Of course, humans cannot use it, since it was not activated like yours. But hopefully some day they will be able to."

"And how do the Anunnaki receive the content of a 'Conduit' to allow them to watch over the humans?" I asked.

"Through the 'Miraya' which we created to function with the Conduit and the An-Hayya'h, even though we felt that you do not deserve it.

The Anunnaki have been watching you, monitoring your activities, listening to your voices, witnessing your wars, your brutality, your greed and indifference towards each other for centuries. We did not interfere, at least not very much."

"But from my experience, you are returning?"

"Yes. We will, because we fear two things that could destroy earth, and annihilate the human race. The domination of earth and the human race by the Grays, and the destruction of human life and the planet Earth at the hands of humans.

The whole earth could blow up. Should this happen, the whole solar system could be destroyed. As we know already, should anything happen to the Moon, the earth will cease to exist."

"Is there hope that we will change?"

"There is always hope. We are trying to change you. The most delightful and comforting aspect of it, is the hope for peace, a brighter future, and a better life that you can accomplish and reach when you discover how to use it without abusing it. Every one of you can do that."

"I wonder how many humans I know will see such change in their lifetime," I said wistfully.

"Even when people die, their An-Hayya'h will always be there for them to use before they depart earth. It will never go away, because it is part of you.

Without it you couldn't exist. Just before you die, your brain activates it for you. Seconds before you die, your mind will project the reenactment of all the events and acts, good and bad, in your entire life, past, and 'zoom' you right toward your next nonphysical destination, where and when you judge yourself, your deeds, and your existence, and where you decide whether you wish to elevate yourself to a higher dimension, or stay in the state of nothingness and loneliness, and for how long. Everything is up to the individual."

"So there is no death. Our minds live forever."

"Indeed, there is no death. Your minds live on, and make all the individual decisions about their future."

"What about reincarnation? Do we return to earth, ever?"

"No, you will not return to earth, nor will your 'soul' migrate to another soul or another body. From the evidence we have garnered, we know and not just believe, that there is no such thing. And why would you wish to return to earth, anyway?

Earth is the lowest sphere of existence for humans; everything else is an improvement!"

"It's good to know that you have not deserted us, Sinhar Inannaschamra. It makes me feel safer, for myself and for humanity."

"My dear Victoria, you are now a full Anunnaki, and you will never, ever, be alone. But I understand your attachment to your previous fellow humans.

There is no reason to worry about them. Humans are always connected to the Anunnaki in this life and the next, and in the future, we plan a much closer communication. So please, go on to your mission with a lighter heart.

There is plenty of bright hope for everyone, even the hybrids, I dare say." I went home, feeling much better about life, the universe, and my mission.

As a matter of fact, I began to look forward to it as a new adventure. And soon I will have a baby girl, too!

*** *** ***

On the Greys interbreeding program with humans

Question from Maxine Walters, Washington, D.C.

Question:
What is the reason behind the Greys interbreeding program with humans?

Answer:
As provided by Sinhar Anbar Anati:
"Very few people, on any planet, really understand the Grays. I have made it my business to learn all I could about them, and I will be able to help you."

"In my trip to their lab, I felt nothing could be worse than these beings," I said. "They seem to me to be a constant menace to everyone."

"They are cruel," said Sinhar Inannaschamra. "But I am thinking about something else. Unless you know their problem, all you see is a technological, highly qualified race without heart or feelings, vicious, violent, and engaged in senseless, merciless experiments. But there is more to it than that. They are a dying civilization, desperately trying to save themselves."

"Dying civilization? How come?" I asked, surprised. With all their activity they seemed very much alive to me, and extremely dangerous.

"Have you ever heard of Progeria? On earth they also call it Hutchinson-Gilford Syndrome, after the two scientists who discovered it in 1886."

"Yes, I have heard a little of it.
Progeria victims are children who age, really become old people, before they even reach puberty. A parent nightmare, but very rare, I should say."

"On earth it is indeed very rare. On average, only one child out of four to eight million births is born with Progeria. It is a rare, and extremely frightening genetic disease, resulting from spontaneous mutation in the sperm or egg of the parents."

"Yes, this is what I have always heard," I said.

"The horror of this disease is that it has no cure. The child is born, starts showing early symptoms, and begins to age right away. The children remain tiny, rarely over four feet, both boys and girls become bald, and all develop a large cranium, a pointy nose and a receding chin, resulting in an amazing resemblance to each other, almost as if they were clones...

And then they die of old age, mostly in their teens but often earlier, and there is nothing anyone can do for them. They develop old age diseases – such as hardening of the arteries – and often die of strokes or coronary disease, while their poor parents have to watch helplessly.

The name Progeria is very appropriate. It means 'before old age,' and expresses it very well."

"But what is the connection of the Progeria children to the Grays?" I asked, a frightening suspicion beginning to form in my mind.

"The civilization of the Grays is millions of years old, and for eons, they have been degenerating. A huge percentage of their population has Progeria, in varying degrees, and because of that, they are threatened with extinction.
No one knows how many Grays are affected, and how many are Progeria-free. We only meet those who are, at least for the present, able to carry on their duties, with the help of their advanced medical technology.
For all we know, there are millions of sick individuals hidden from view on their home planet."

"This is incredible," I said, shuddering.

"You must also remember that the Grays do not reproduce sexually. They used to, but not anymore. Also, they don't reproduce like the Anunnaki, either. For thousands of years, they have been relying on cloning.
And that has damaged their DNA even further, creating more and more cases of Progeria. They are dying out."

"An entire civilization destroyed by Progeria...it is almost impossible to believe," I said.

"If you study the two groups, you will see strong similarities between the Grays and Progeria children. I won't go

into all of them, as the list could go on for days, but let's consider the most prominent ones.
For one thing, Progeria does not produce any form of dementia.

Both groups maintain their excellent mental faculties, usually with high IQ, until they die. That is a very important clue, but here are the others for your consideration:

- Neither group ever grows much beyond four feet.
- Both have fragile, weak bodies, with thin arms and legs; all their bones are thin, as a general rule.
- Both groups are bald.
- Grays have no sexual reproduction, most have no genitalia at all. Progeria children never reach puberty.
- Both have large heads by comparison to their bodies.
- Both have receding chins and pointy noses. Within their groups, they closely resemble each other. The Grays are cloned; the Progeria children look as if they could have been cloned.

"So will the experiments they do help them survive?"

"That is what they hope for. They take the eggs and the sperm from humans and combine them with Grays' DNA. Thus, they create the Hybrid children."

"Those poor children. I pity them so."

"They are not exactly what you think, Victoria. I pity them too, but you must realize that they are closer to the Grays in their character and behavior than they are to humans."

"What are they like?"

"The first generation Hybrids are smaller than human children. They tend to follow the growth pattern of the Gray parent – and by now you know this is a very fragile one. They are even smaller than Progeria babies.
The retardation of growth begins before birth."

"When you say 'first generation" does it mean that they go on mixing the genetic material?"

"Yes, that is exactly what they do. The Hybrids may or may not have Progeria, but naturally, the more human DNA that is mixed into the species, the more chances there are of eliminating the bad genes. So they breed the Hybrids with more human DNA, always hoping to eradicate the disease, never quite succeeding. That is why they have to get fresh human specimens all the time."

"Do you think they have a chance of survival?"

"No, personally I don't think they have a chance. I think they are doomed. But many Anunnaki disagree with me. At any rate, there is nothing we can do either way."

"Do you think the authorities on earth know about all that? Like the governments of various countries? Why isn't something being done about it?"

Sinhar Inannaschamra looked at me silently. Her big black Anunnaki eyes were suddenly full of such sorrow, such deep sadness, that I did not know how to react. Finally she said, "Yes, they do know. I have to tell you the truth, Victoria, even though it breaks my heart to do so. Almost all earth governments have made a deal with the Grays. They supply them with humans."

I jumped on my feet, completely horrified. "They do that? They sell humans to the Grays for torture and killing? What do they gain?"

"Can't you guess?" said Sinhar Inannaschamra quietly. "The Grays give them the technology they crave. They have learned so much from the Grays, and they mostly use it for military purposes. Humans are not kind to each other. Look at all the wars, torture, genocide, holocausts... all part of human history, and still taking place."

"Unfortunately, this is true," I said.

"Anyway, there are various places on earth where these activities can be studied, such as military bases, mostly located underground, in many countries. Some day you will spend some time there, I am sure."

"Well," I said, trying to recover from the shock. "I can't answer for the earth's governments, but I can try to help."

"Indeed you can. We are trying, in many ways, to alleviate the situation, even though, as I've explained before, we cannot police the whole universe, or even the entire earth."

"Do you think I should go and take a look at the Hybrids, as part of my education?"

"Yes, I think the best thing to do would be to take you on a field trip. You must meet these Hybrids face to face before you make your decision about the mission. But there is something else I wanted to talk to you about. This mission will have to be on earth, you know.
There are no Hybrid bases anywhere else, certainly not on Ashtari. You will be alone for long periods.
We don't go back and forth to earth very often, which means that you will have to spend years on earth, except from short vacations."

"Marduchk told me he had committed himself to work with those apelike creatures he shape-shifted into, and scared me so much after our wedding. That means, I am sure, that he will be away for extended periods of time as well, doesn't it?"

"Yes, that is how we all live. My husband is on missions all the time. Most of us are. I used to go to distant places, also, even though currently my mission is teaching fulltime at the Academy."

"But are Marduchk and I going to be completely isolated from each other for all these years?"

"No, of course not. Now that you have your Conduit opened, you can talk to each other every single day you spend apart, and every few years, you can meet for a vacation."

"That does not sound too bad," I said. "I will miss Marduchk and all of you very much, but what are a few years? You have given me the hope of living a very long and useful life, and Marduchk has begun to teach me about the next phase of eternity, which is not yet entirely clear to me but very comforting, nonetheless. I am trying very hard to absorb it all.

In that light, I would be willing to make the effort without any regrets. There is only one thing... I am not sure if you will think it is a good idea..."

"I can sense what it is, Victoria. You want a child."

"Was I that transparent?"

"It was to be expected. Anyone who has had to give a baby up for adoption, the way you so heroically did, would want another baby. That is only natural. But why shouldn't you? Why did you think it an idea that would not appeal to me?"

"Because I would have to leave the child on Nibiru when I finally go on the mission. Another abandonment."

"First of all, you did not abandon your son. You insisted on knowing all the conditions, you were assured of the loving family and wonderful future he was going to have. And as for the next child, surely you see that our system here is extremely family oriented.

When you go on your mission, let's say when the child is somewhere between five and ten, you will have an entire family ready to take over.

Think about it – the baby's father, aunt, uncle, nieces, and not to mention her loving great-great-great-grandmother ten times removed, namely me – will all be there, loving this child.

And you can talk to the baby every single day through the Miraya, see each other during vacations, and come back long before the child graduates from the Academy.

I don't think your mission will take seventy-one years, and frankly, I see no abandonment issues here at all."

"What will Marduchk think?"

"He would probably love the idea! He likes children. Not all Anunnaki choose to have children, you know. Some never do, some only have one or two and then spend thousands of years without further reproduction.

It's entirely a matter of free will. Those who want children are of course encouraged to have them whenever they please, since they make excellent parents. Those who do not wish to raise children are never pressured into having them.

And remember, Victoria, you can have more children after you come back from your mission, if you choose to do so.

It is always your choice, and time does not play any part in it."

I was quiet for a few minutes. Being raised on earth had eroded so much of the self-confidence and poise all Anunnaki possess. Well, I will have to work on becoming more like them, that is all.

"This time I will have the baby Anunnaki style," I said, feeling better every minute, "in the tube. So I can freely study and travel during the time before it is ready for its birth."

"Incidentally, you can decide in advance if you want a boy or a girl," said Sinhar Inannaschamra, matter of factly.

"I'll consult Marduchk about that," I said. "He may have a preference. I don't care if it is a boy or a girl. I just want a healthy baby."

"Well, that is a given. You will have a perfect baby, every time. And tomorrow, come back and I'll take you on the field trip. I think meeting the Hybrids will be a very interesting experience."

I went home, and as I was waiting for Marduchk to come back from the Akashic Library, I strolled in the garden, breathing in the evening air and the scent of the opening night blooming flowers. I saw Marduchk approaching and waved at him.

"You got your Conduit opened!" he said right away. "I can sense it."

"Indeed," I said. "Shall we try to communicate telepathically? Let's see if I am good at it."

"Do you know how to start it?" asked Marduchk.

"I do." I did something in my mind, which regrettably I cannot explain to anyone who has not activated their Conduit, and the Conduit opened, first a little hesitantly, then fully. It was a surprisingly easy, extremely pleasant and effortless way to conduct a conversation.

I related to Marduchk everything that happened, in detail, and a conversation that would have taken about an hour was accomplished in a few minutes.

As for the great decision (namely the child, not the mission), Marduchk was charmed by the idea. "A daughter," he communicated, meditatively, "if you don't mind. I had two sons, but I have never had a daughter… it would be a nice experience."

"Fine with me," I communicated back. "And when I come back, we might consider having more. I love children."

"Certainly, if you wish," Marduchk communicated. "I find raising children extremely nice." And so the decision was made, and I felt very, very happy.

This is a good time to explain something regarding Anunnaki fatherhood. Earth readers might wonder how the Anunnaki male feels about children, since he does not contribute sperm, and the fertilization of the eggs, as I have explained in a previous chapter, occurs by the activation of the specialized light.

Does the Anunnaki male see himself as the father to his wife's natural children?

The answer is a resounding "yes."

The Anunnaki do not put much weight on trifling physical matters, such as the use of sperm. The Anunnaki couple is an inseparable unit, and whichever way a child comes into their lives, the child is secure of a having a loving father. I wish the same could be said of all human fathers – whether they do or do not contribute sperm.

*** *** ***

Are the Anunnaki going to take over Earth?

Questions by Reverend Nancy Santos.

Question : Is one of these Anunnaki Gods going to take over the earth after the pole shift?

Answer:
No! For two reasons:
- **1**-The pole is not going to shift. So don't worry. This is based upon mainstream science. However, it could shift as it did before, millions of years ago. But scientists are not concerned. They are absolutely sure that no shift will occur anytime soon.
- **2**- If the Anunnaki intend to take over Earth, they will not wait until the pole shift. They can do it any time, at will. But they are not interested at all.

Read the section on the final warning.

Dear Sandra, you have to remember that the Anunnaki are not territorial. Besides, planet Earth is meaningless to them. We, as human beings are not interesting enough to the Anunnaki. Our natural resources are found on numerous planets, readily accessible to the Anunnaki.

There are 7 galaxies in the cosmos filled with natural resources available to the Anunnaki, and these resources are not contaminated.

We think that we are the center of the universe, because we are arrogant and pretentious.

In fact, very very very few alien civilizations are aware of our existence. And they have no interest whatsoever of paying a visit to us.

However, and according to Stephen William Hawking, it is not a good idea to try to reach other civilizations in the universe. He warned us. Now, this does not mean that other alien races are not visiting our planet. Some have visited Earth several times, as part of their galactic excursions.

They came and they left. Nevertheless, the intraterrestrial aliens are still here.

Why?

It is very simple: They lived here millions of years before we were created. This is why we call them the intraterrestrials. They are not humans, and they live in isolated areas and aquatic habitats. These races are peaceful to a certain degree, as long as, the human race will not jeopardize the safety of Earth.

So in conclusion, the Anunnaki are not going to take over the Earth. But please do remember, that we are expecting a global communication/contact/rapport with them in 2022.

*** *** ***

Human race: The Anunnaki creation of a new human race after 2022

Question by Raoul Mondragon, Vera Cruz, Mexico.

Question: I am very worried by what you have written on the subject of the return of the Anunnaki in 2022? Is it for real? Are they going to change the way we look? Are they going to get rid of us and replace us with a new human race? What kind?

Answer:
What kind of a new human race are we talking about?
A new genetic race?
A bio-genetic race?
A new race with new physical characteristics and different physiognomy?
"None of the above," said the Honorable Master Li.
He added verbatim, word for word, and unedited: "The physical form of humans will not change.
Unless, the Anunnaki will take us back to the primordial Chimiti (Akkadian word for the genetic lab tubes, used by the Anunnaki to create an early form of human beings.)
And this is very unlikely, even impossible. The changes will occur on different levels, and almost instantly."

*** *** ***

Anunnaki Prevention of Use of Nuclear Weapons

Question by A. D

Question: Will the Anunnaki intervene to prevent possible aggressive use of atomic/thermonuclear weapons against other nation(s) prior to, and/or during their return in 2022?

Benazir Bhutto

Answer:
The most imminent threat will come not from Iran, but from Pakistan, an as yet highly unlikely surprise scenario.
Benazir Bhutto knew of this, spoke about it behind closed doors, and was assassinated soon after.

I find it very childish and ridiculous when American ufologists wrote on subjects pertaining to extraterrestrials and nuclear issues since they are absolute outsiders.
Nowhere in their books have they ever written on the Anunnaki and their Ba'abs.
Why are some of the Ba'abs so extremely important?
They lead to the parallel dimensions of the Anunnaki, and the beginning of time, where the God-Particle/Higgs Boson can be found, which is the reason for the building of CERN's Large Hadron Collider (LHC).

Through the Miraya – a cosmic screen/monitor with a vast depot of data that informs the Anunnaki of past, present and future events occurring in non-linear form, and in different galaxies by which the Anunnaki can monitor the activities of humans on Earth, the Grays, Reptilians, Nordics, Lyrans, Dracos, Plaeidians etc, and envoys from various other galactic civilizations wrongly identified and referred to as "The Galactic Federation/Council".

*** *** ***

There is no way for a medium/channeler/psychic to the stars sitting in his/her apartment in Wala Wala, or Biloxi, Mississippi or in the swamps of Louisiana, listening to Willie Nelson's "On the Road Again" to access this Miraya and reveal the secrets of the Universe.
The Anunnaki will definitely intervene if a nuclear explosion were seen on the Miraya screen to happen near a Ba'ab connected to their galaxy, close to the membrane of the Universe that could cause chaos and disequilibrium in the eleventh dimension of the Universe.

This is very possible, since the speech given by Adolf Hitler at the 1936 Berlin Olympics, can still be heard in different worlds, as can the Sermon that was given by Yeshuah (Jesus) on the Mount of Olives.
Both can be heard in the "Time-Space Depository".

A bank of information, that Nikola Tesla accidentally tapped into.

*** *** ***

Nikola Tesla

American history has been unfair to Tesla and given his credits to the greedy and egotistical Edison.
Everyone on the planet using A/C electricity today should give thanks and praise to Nikola Tesla and not Thomas Edison.

Only humans on earth refer to space-time.

All other extraterrestrial sentient beings use the term time-space to define the limits of the known universe.

*** *** ***

Who will survive the return of the Anunnaki?

Question: What percentage of the world's population will survive the return of the Anunnaki, to become part of the new human race after 2022?

Answer:
Calculate the dimensions of the Ziggurat of Enki in Ur (in Iraq), to find the number of earth's population that would survive which had been predicted millennia ago.
And all this while he looked out from the window of his Manhattan apartment at eight fifteen in the morning, after a late night - no an all night interview.

*** *** ***

How many other Anunnaki will be part of the return?

Question: Though the return will be led by Sinhars Marduchk and Inannaschamra, how many other Anunnaki will be part of the return?
And how many Anunnaki guides will there be, for humans who will be saved and returned to earth after the cleansing?
Answer:
That is a very normal way for a purely human mind to ask such a question. The truth is: the galactic mind of the extraterrestrials functions differently.

Consequently, the alien mode of operation becomes totally incomprehensible to our mind, and instead of focusing on how many military personnel they might send, we should focus on how many I.S.M.s they will operate at close proximity to Earth. This stands for "Intelligent Satellite Module".

Each module is approximately 8ft to 10ft in diameter, made of "fibro-metal", an alloy of elements not found on Earth, which is cone shaped on the top half and oval shaped on the bottom half.

Worth mentioning here, the Gray aliens have craft similar to the "I.S.M." being smaller in diameter at 6ft to 8ft wide.

These were witnessed by farmers in the mid-west several times, and reported on cable T.V. The purpose of the Gray's I.S.Ms, was to scan particular areas in the United States for several military strategic reasons, such as creating an atmospheric shield network which could alter the fabric of weather and be used to control climatic/atmospheric conditions over a chosen area/country.

This military ecological weapon system produces tsunamis, earthquakes, mysterious underground detonations, complete destruction of all types of agriculture, forests and natural resources (crops, trees, orchards, and every kind of plant).

Have we seen these kinds of catastrophic events recently in different parts of the world?

Whilst the Gray I.S.Ms require a complicated operational structure, encompassing large numbers of military personnel, one Anunnaki can handle up to one thousand of their I.S.M. machines.

They will be using the Shabka - a cosmic net, made up of anti-radar emissions and rays that not even N.O.R.A.D. can detect. The Gray/Earth joint program I.S.M.'s are detectable and clearly visible to the naked eye, whilst the Anunnaki I.S.Ms are totally invisible and completely undetectable, as they jump from one time-space pocket to another.

Worth mention here to all our readers: The difference between "time-space" travel and "space-time" travel is this: In the mode of time-space, the human mind cannot yet understand it, nor can the eyes see it, as we do not yet fully comprehend the concept of time. In space-mode time however, human eyes can glimpse the craft, for a split second before it vanishes/jumps to another pocket. Only in this instance, does the space-time appear linearly to humans.

One Anunnaki I.S.M. module is capable of covering up to 9,000 square miles.

These mini-spaceship machines will be interconnected through a massive net of rays that will seal off the Earth's atmosphere when the Anunnaki return.

The number of Anunnaki who will be operating this return mission is as yet unknown. Very few Anunnaki personnel will be needed to operate this enterprise.

When this massive net of rays is interwoven, it forms a dark gray gluey substance that appears to us as a blend of burning metal, bark and rubber with the most awful foul odor imaginable!! The ghastly and noxious odor itself is enough to kill people.

Light from the sun will be completely blocked out, as this gluey substance, known to the Anunnaki as "Zafta", forms a solid egg-shell-like casing around the entire planet from which there will be no escape.

This will truly be the end of the world, and life on Earth as we know it."

It is not going to happen!!

I will be inviting all of you to a big banquet come January 1st 2013 in Acapulco, Mexico with free Margaritas and Bloody Mary's cocktails to go round till the sun goes down – no cover charge!!

*** *** ***

Efficient energy systems of the Anunnaki.

Question: What kind of clean and efficient energy systems, and modes of transportation will the Anunnaki introduce after 2022?
Answer:

After the cleansing is done, no oil, coal, natural gas, or any other carbon based fuels will be used to power any car, machinery or mechanical equipment/apparatus.

Energy to power all of the above will be provided via satellites which harness cosmic energy.

By then even solar energy will be regarded as an archaic and rudimentary form of harnessing energy.

This will be made possible by the process of opening the Anunnaki cosmic Ba'abs, which are also the stargates to multiple dimensions.

Eleven of these Ba'abs exist, within the multi-dimensional cosmic landscape, adjacent to Earth.

*** *** ***

Signs before the return of the Anunnaki

Question: What are the signs that people will see in the skies the day before the Anunnaki return, and where will they be seen?

Answer:
One year before the return of the Anunnaki, around the end of the year 2021, the governments of many countries will start to circulate publications and manuals describing signs that will indicate the appearance 0f extraterrestrial craft visible to the public at large.

I am absolutely convinced that many Bishops and Archbishops in the United States and England have already been briefed on the subject, and were secretly asked to cooperate on the redaction of material that would suit religious dogma with "intelligent design" as well as the frightening arrival of extraterrestrials to our planet.

Ironically, four major Anunnaki stargates will be activated and opened, which religious leaders will also interpret as the arrival of the "Four Horsemen" as stated in the Book of Revelation, and will be urging believers to run to their churches and pray.

Readers and believers of the "Left Behind" series will have another shot at redemption…(Not!!)

Meanwhile, from the end of 2021 to November 30th, 2022 American citizens will have the most unusual evacuation display of UFOs/USOs of all shapes and sizes (oval, circular, crescent-shaped, triangular, cylindrical and every other shape witnessed, reported and ridiculed by the media, military disinformers and debunkers alike.) These are the vehicles of the Gray aliens jointly operated with the military.

*** *** ***

Anunnaki's "tool of annihilation"

Question: Who/what created the "tool of annihilation" that the Anunnaki will use when they return?

Answer:
The "Tool of Annihilation" was created by the Majlas – the Anunnaki High Council, as stated by Sinhar Anbar Anati, specifically for the purpose of cleansing the earth from all its contamination upon their return in 2022.

This tool of annihilation will be utilized in the event of hostile situations, where uninformed rednecks (Back in the saddle again) and other surburbanites will pull out their hunting rifles and shotguns to shoot at spaceships belonging to the most advanced race in the known universe. Those are the ones who are going to get it first!

*** *** ***

Books by Maximillien de Lafayette

1520 Things You Don't Know about UFOs, Aliens Technology, Extraterrestrials and U.S. Black Operations. Vol.1.

Volume 1 from a set of 2 volumes. Third Edition.
The importance of this groundbreaking book resides in the originality of its material and world-premiere information on UFOs, USOs, extraterrestrials, intraterrestrials, aliens, alien technology, U.S. black operations and aliens multiple universes, not readily available elsewhere, and covering the most important events and findings in the history of modern ufology and the study of alien civilization, parallel universes, and multiple dimensions, as DIRECTLY explained to us by the extraterrestrials we met with since 1947.

Nowhere, in any published book, on websites, in conferences and other published material, you will ever find the information, data, briefings and reports provided in this book.
For instance (Information and reports never revealed before or known to ufologists and the general public):
1. Complex machines used by the aliens to talk to us

2. Transcripts of our meetings with aliens and extraterrestrials
3. Secret Presidential Memoranda about UFOs and extraterrestrials
4. Deciphering aliens' codes and languages (Alien Phonology)
5. The secret Alien language lexicon
6. Photos and lists of names of American, British, French, and Russian linguists who worked on deciphering aliens' symbols and scientists who worked on alien reverse engineering/technology
7. Manufactured aliens: Extraterrestrials manufacture themselves, and are born fully grown and mature
8. Categories of alien races and their organism structure
9. Mode of operation of UFOs and aliens time-machines
10. Mode of communication with aliens (Exopherom)
11. Extraterrestrial Mind/Cellular Motor. How an alien brain is wired?
12. What happened at the first meeting with the aliens?
13. Meeting with three different non-human species
14. The Grays' world
15. Aliens explanation of the Universe, Time, Space, Parallel dimensions, Creation of the world and human species
16. Mind-bending technology and weapons systems we got from the aliens
17. Corridor Plasma
18. Aliens cellular memory
19. Technology that could rewind, stop or accelerate time
20. Technology that could transport cities from one continent to another
21. Locations of Stargates around the globe
22. Hidden entrances to other worlds and dimensions
23. Mind-blowing Black Operations and Projects that will change humanity's future and our place in the universe
And much more!- Dina Vitantonio, Editor.

1520 Things You Don't Know about UFOs, Aliens Technology, Extraterrestrials and U.S. Black Operations. Vol.2.

In this volume:
1. The Grays and the BL-rm3
2. 4 UFOs crashes on record
3. Human bodies' parts were found inside an alien spacecraft
4. Excerpts from the Aliens Transcripts of our meetings with extraterrestrials and intraterrestrials in 1947 and 1948
5. Scientist and Nobel Prize winner, Dr. Francis Crick wrote: "The astonishing hypothesis is, that there is no soul." This is exactly what the aliens told the military.
6. What the aliens told us about Jesus, the disciples, the four Bibles and the Gnostics.
7. Aliens Rewinding Time Technology
8. Translation Signals Box (TSB): A machine the aliens gave us, which allowed us to respond to their communications and messages
9. CTF (Transmission Channel): A device used by military scientists to receive messages from aliens
10. The Web: A network of underwater channels linking together intraterrestrial communities
11. VCP: Vortex Tunnel Weapon System
12. The military has successfully sent some of its personnel through a vortex tunnel to another dimension, and successfully, they were brought back
13. Aliens Spinning Mobile Satellite" (SMS): The mode of transportation down the underwater bases
14. Corridor Plasma and the Vacuum Tunnel: Underwater cold plasma tunnel used by the intraterrestrials (The Grays) to navigate underwater
15. Bioelectric extraterrestrial robots "B.E.R": Human-like robots capable of acting like human beings
16. Aliens zooming into the past and jumping into the future
17. BCB: The Aliens Compressor Machine
18. List of names of scientists who collaborated with aliens and/or worked on alien reverse engineering
19. Major discoveries based on alien technology
20. Non-disclosure policy by Catholic archbishops and secret committees. (Their names and role)
21. On Presidents Truman, Eisenhower, Nixon and Bush Sr. knowledge of and involvement with the alien phenomenon.
22. The shipped aliens' dead bodies to Walter Reed Hospital

NEW Maria Orsic, Nikola Tesla, Their Extraterrestrials Messages, The Occult And UFOs (In 2 Volumes)

MARIA ORSIC IS THE MOST IMPORTANT PERSONALITY IN UFOLOGY'S HISTORY!!

3rd Edition, totally revised, updated and indexed. Volume 1 (278 Pages. A huge file of 27 MB) from a set of 2 volumes. This book is also available in paperback in 2 volumes at Lulu.com A world premiere! A must read book. Absolutely fascinating!!!! The world's first book on Maria Orsic and the Ladies of Vril, and Nikola Tesla's extraterrestrials' connection. Hundreds upon hundreds of photos, drawings and sketches from the original files. Information from secrets files of the NKVD, KGB, OSS, Gestapo, SS, MI5, and intelligence agencies in 6 countries. Everything began with Maria Orsic, including extraterrestrial messages, aliens' contacts and the UFOs in modern times.

The UFO phenomenon, the first contacts with aliens from civilizations beyond our solar system, and extraterrestrials' messages, all started with an occult-metaphysical-mysticism-psychical movement created by Maria Orsic in 1917, a medium and founder of the Vrilerinnen (The Vril Society), and based upon messages she received from extraterrestrials from Aldebaran (Alpha Tauri), which contained technical data and precise instructions on how to build a super "Out of this World" flying machine (UFO). But of course everything changed as soon as the SS took control of the metaphysical efforts of Orsic and her

associates. And the macabre episode ended with the SS senior officers slaughtering 60 German scientists who were working on the final prototypes of the Bell UFO, when they became convinced that Germany has lost the war. Fearing that their UFO technology will fall into the hands of the Red Army, SS officers shot the leading engineers. And those who managed to escape, just 3 days before the Russian troops entered Berlin, vanished from the face of the earth, taking with them the most important documents and blueprints of the last versions of their Bell-UFOs, stealth supersonic bombers, jet-fighters, and other secret miracle-weapons. But the greatest, most unique and most formidable person in all these scenarios, Germany's UFOs saga, and the history of ufology and extraterrestrials' contacts was and still is Maria Orsic. Maria was an extraordinary woman on so many levels!
Read about:

1. Life and times of Maria Orsic. The first person on Earth to receive extraterrestrial messages in 1917. The first woman to build a UFO using technical data given to her by extraterrestrials
2. Unusual medium/psychic with unusual friends and extraterrestrials from Aldebaran.
3. Maria Orsic, Anunnaki and Sumerians link
4. Explanation of the aliens' messages Maria received in Sumerian-Ugaritic-Ana'kh cuneiform scripts
5. The story of the German UFOs
6. The extraterrestrials who survived the Great Flood
7. Shortcut to others planets, stars and galaxies
8. Stargates: The stairways to the heavens
9. Himmler SS attempts to kill Maria Orsic
10. Brüder Des Lichts
11. Thule-Gesellschaft
12. Vril-Gesellschaft
13. Description of life on Adelbaran
14. Profile of the Adelbaran's extraterrestrials
15. Comparison between Adelbaran and Ash.Ta.Ri (Nibiru)
16. Germany's first Bell-UFOs
17. The paranormal aspect of the German UFOs
18. UFOs, Aliens, Aliens' Rapture, Nikola Tesla, and the United States Government
19. Nicola Tesla's files on extraterrestrials
20. J. Edgar Hoover and FBI Tesla's files
21. Tesla, Brigadier General L. C. Craigie, and Patterson Air Force Base, and the "Project Nick"

22.Russian Telsa's beam weapon system and the United States Strategic Defense Initiative (SDI)
23.Tesla Teslascope; device to contact extraterrestrials

*** *** ***

The author can be reached at
Delafayette6@aol.com

Published by
Times Square Press
New York, New York, USA

Printed in the United States of America
April 2012

Made in the USA
Middletown, DE
09 August 2019